SOARING THROUGH ADVERSITY

LIFE LESSONS TO LEAD, TRIUMPH, AND RISE ABOVE

Ken,
Continue to soar &
rise above!
Renee J Breazeale

RENEE J. BREAZEALE

SPARK PUBLICATIONS
Charlotte, North Carolina

Soaring through Adversity—
Life Lessons to Lead, Triumph, and Rise Above
Renee Johnson Breazeale

Designed, produced, and published by SPARK Publications
SPARKpublications.com
Charlotte, North Carolina

Edited by Sherre' L. DeMao, CGS

Printed in the United States of America

Paperback, October 2022, ISBN: 978-1-953555-33-5
Hardback, October 2022, ISBN: 978-1-953555-39-7
Ebook, November 2022, ISBN: 978-1-953555-35-9

Library of Congress Control Number: 2022916218

DEDICATION

I dedicate this book to my daughters, Heather and Savannah; my bonus daughters, Madison and Jordan; my granddaughters, Lexy and Charleigh; and my bonus granddaughters, Kali, Layla, and Violet.

May you find strength and encouragement through my life's adversities and lessons. May you understand that with faith, you too can experience the boundless opportunities to soar at whatever you attempt in life.

TABLE OF CONTENTS

CHAPTER 1
Small Town, Big Dreams ... 11

CHAPTER 2
Broke, Not Broken ... 17

CHAPTER 3
It's a Man's World ... 25

CHAPTER 4
Countdown to Liftoff ... 31

CHAPTER 5
Dream in Motion ... 39

CHAPTER 6
I Do! I Don't! ... 45

CHAPTER 7
Victory Is Mine ... 53

CHAPTER 8
Neonatal Miracle ... 61

CHAPTER 9
Furiously Paddling ... 67

CHAPTER 10
Making Waves ... 77

CHAPTER 11
Growing Pains ... 83

CHAPTER 12
Victory Is Sweet ... 89

CHAPTER 13
Backup Plan ... 97

CHAPTER 14
A Taxing Situation ... 101

CHAPTER 15
Place to Call Home ... 109

CHAPTER 16
Culture Clash ... 115

CHAPTER 17
Uni-Screwed ... 121

CHAPTER 18
War Zone ... 129

CHAPTER 19
Third Time's a Charm ... 135

CHAPTER 20
Jumping Ship ... 141

CHAPTER 21
Stopped in My Tracks ... 147

CHAPTER 22
Walk, Can't Run ... 157

CHAPTER 23
Starting Over ... 163

CHAPTER 24
Avoiding the Bunker Mentality ... 169

CHAPTER 25
Crisis Advantage ... 173

CHAPTER 26
Kicking & Screaming ... 177

CHAPTER 27
Losing My Identity ... 183

CHAPTER 28
Finding My Why ... 189

About the Author ... 194
You Don't Haveto Soar Alone ... 196
Acknowledgments ... 197
Soar with Renee ... 200

INTRODUCTION

A brain tumor has a way of putting things into perspective. My brain tumor became one of the great blessings in my life and I have shared this countless times with others since it happened. Why, you may ask?

I spent most of my career declaring, "My name is Renee Johnson Breazeale, and I am a workaholic," wearing it almost like a badge of honor. My thirty-two-year entrepreneurial journey to "prove I could" was an addiction for me. It took a toll on many aspects of my life, including my health, but I was determined to succeed no matter what. From a broken back to a softball-sized brain tumor that left me unable to walk, I began to understand the importance of a balanced life, a life experienced fully, and a life that was not just about the work that I did.

Don't wait for life-altering circumstances to properly align your priorities. If this book helps you know that there is more to you than what you do for a living, I will be grateful. There's so much more to life and living than any of us fully realize.

Let me ask you this: Do you believe in being in the right place at the right time? Or do you believe in divine intervention? I have learned in my life to consider my gut feelings and the peace that comes from making the right choices. For me, personal decisions are best when they are divinely guided.

I have never regretted the choices I've made in my life. I believe they were not a coincidence and that all that I have endured and needed to overcome was God's more excellent plan for my life. Even more uniquely designed was the peace that overwhelmed me with each decision that birthed the next opportunity and chapter of my life.

This is why I knew I had to write this book. What happens when you take the leap toward what you believe is your life's purpose, only to find out they were not the plans intended for your best life? These are times when you must be diligent in your thoughts and be deliberate in each step you take. I believe we don't create our purpose; we discover and pursue it one step at a time. It is moving forward in faith. It is determination in action.

I knew as time went on that it would never be about the money, a title, or things. I found my passion by discovering the gifts God gave me. This revelation would lead me down an unexpected path, to a life of extraordinary adventures and opportunities to help others. I have learned through the years that by using my faith and a servant's mentality and heart, I could build a business of substance that would represent much more than just a strong financial statement through "giving back" along the way. During my journey of highs and lows, I felt the most fulfilled when I concentrated on what I could do to give to others rather than what I could achieve on my own.

Looking back over the adversities that came my way, I would learn that while that was the path God set me on, He never said this journey would be easy. I would come to understand that a seemingly easy jump-start doesn't mean there will not be bumps along the road. However, the plans designed for me were more extensive than I could have imagined. These bumps were there to lift me to higher ground for a better view of what lay ahead. Perseverance and faith, not perfection, helped me maintain hope in my dream.

It was through my faith that I also found great inspiration from the symbolism behind the bald eagle. It is why it became the icon of my company, and the verse Isaiah 40:31 was the foundation we operated under. For me, the eagle has represented courage and being fearless in actions, not just in words. The tenacity of an eagle to be relentless in its pursuit, keeping its eyes on the prize with extraordinary vision, symbolized victory always being within one's sight, even amidst blinding obstacles. The faithfulness of an eagle and the way it nurtures its young symbolized always knowing you were not alone and seeing a way to make the pathway and journey easier for those that followed.

You may not have experienced the same adversities that I have, but I am sure you have had your own hardships and struggles. Perhaps they were short-lived, and other times they may have seemed never-ending. Whatever you are going through, you can rise above, like an eagle with divine direction in your life.

Whether what I was experiencing was purposeful, powerful, or painful, these adventures formed me to be the person I am today. I know it sounds crazy to many, but I wouldn't change a thing. Would I have done some things differently? Yes, absolutely! That's not regret. That's wisdom. But the ultimate outcomes were by design and created for my best life. I lived and I learned, and now it's time to share.

My hope and prayer are that when you read this, you understand things don't always turn out as you planned, but they do work out for your best plan if you just have a little faith. I hope this book will help you speak up, stand up, and step up to pave the way for others to succeed with passion and purpose right alongside you.

Most of all, I hope this book will help you know you can soar through any adversity, like an eagle flying high above the storm.

"But those who trust in the LORD will find new strength. They will soar high on wings like eagles. They will run and not grow weary. They will walk and not faint."

—Isaiah 40:31

"Life is a
collection of
lessons learned
for opportunities
to grow."

CHAPTER 1

SMALL TOWN, BIG DREAMS

It all begins in a tiny town called Marshville, North Carolina, which was also playfully known by all my friends growing up as "Marshvegas." Why? Because it wasn't anything like Las Vegas. It was the extreme opposite! It had two stoplights, no fast food, no movie theater, not even a skating rink. The major highlight in this town of 2,500 citizens was the annual fall carnival and street fair known as the Boll Weevil Festival. This was our excitement with music, street food vendors, and the small carnival rides.

My life began as normal as most. While my parents worked hard to make a better life for our family, as an only child, I took on a great deal of responsibility at a young age. I didn't mind. And looking back, I see how it built my character and taught me never to take anything for granted.

My parents owned a textile manufacturing company that employed most of my family and others in the community. It was flourishing—at first, that is. At a young age, I could see the pride that my parents displayed in having their own business. They enjoyed impacting their family, other employees and their families, and the community. Even when times were hard, they continued to maintain their positive relationships and quality reputation. It gave them a sense of purpose and belonging in our community.

They specialized in making the fabric used in women's apparel for large clothing designers in New York. I can quite vividly remember the designers' numerous visits to tour the plant and meet with my parents. They would surprise me with custom-made specially designed little matching skirts and jackets made from the fabric my parents produced. These outfits were unlike anything I had ever seen, much less worn. I looked like a tiny businessperson, and I did nothing but complain about how uncomfortable they were to wear. I would have rather been in my play clothes. Plus, my parents were busy building their business and every extra penny went toward keeping it alive. My clothes were simple and comfortable—nothing fancy. I didn't need these clothes to make me or my parents feel good about ourselves.

While it might have seemed like a nice gesture, these gifts made me feel like I wasn't good enough. As I look back on this time in my life, I see these designers as people who wanted to change us into what they thought we should be. The dinners in these outfits were not only uncomfortable for me, but they were also long and grueling and stressful on my parents because these people were so very different from us and were only interested in what my parents had to offer them. My parents' factory in this small southern town allowed the designers to purchase fabric at much cheaper prices than their competitors in the North—increasing their profit margin. Even with this advantage, that still wasn't enough. No matter the relationship they appeared to have forged, or how much better the quality of the fabric, my parents were continually forced to take their pricing lower and lower until there was barely enough left for my parents to run the company.

Pricing pressure from New York wasn't the only stress my parents were managing in the business. The overall market segment was narrowing quickly as imports overtook the industry, driving prices even lower. It got to a point where my parents could no longer compete. Rather than giving up, they reinvented themselves and poured all their earnings back into ways to keep the business alive. They transformed their company into manufacturing upholstery only, but soon thereafter many textile factories moved to Mexico for cheaper labor and production costs. Soon similar upholstery began arriving from China even though the quality was inferior, but the pricing was lower than anyone had ever seen. Like my parent's company, all US manufacturers suffered. My parents worked so hard only to lose it all in the end.

The Trailer Park Becomes Home

Subsequently, we moved out of our brick home in to the trailer park across town so my parents could make ends meet. Growing up, I was no stranger to this park. I visited this trailer park regularly. I would ride my bike across town to see my grandmother and aunt. I didn't come from a wealthy family, just a family of love who worked hard to make a better life. For me, at nine years old, I was OK with it, but my parents were devastated and felt like they had failed.

My parents would tell me that one of their biggest mistakes was not understanding the value they provided to their customer to be able to express why they were worthy of the price they were asking. They allowed their customers to make them feel insignificant, and no one benefited in the long term. As I grew older, these conversations with my parents and the visits and attitudes of the people that thought they were superior to my parents shaped how I would approach business. At the time, I didn't realize that what had happened to them would impact and influence me for the rest of my life.

My parents' company did not make it, but they have always been winners in my eyes. My mom took a sales position, and my dad stuck with his background in the textile industry. We never got back to the brick house or affluent neighborhood, but we went from a small trailer to a manufactured house on a piece of land that my parents have made improvements to along the way and still live in today.

Getting Out of "Marshvegas"

Because of my parents' early struggles, I became very independent through taking on a lot of responsibility at an early age. Being an only child around adults most of the time, I learned so much from watching them persevere. Looking back, I know that is where I got my personal determination and work ethic.

Throughout my childhood, the more my parents worked, the more I found myself alone. I was doing chores around the house very early as a way to help lift some responsibilities they were juggling. It was as early as the age of ten that I could feel the stress they were carrying, and I wanted to help in any way that I could. For me, I believe that this early urge to help make things better led to me wanting to fix or solve everyone's problems most of my life. At a young age, I was taught a high level of independence that would prove to be both good and bad. There are times when you need to depend on others to help, and I would learn that fact the hard way later in life.

When they weren't working their day jobs, my parents were also musicians. It was a way of enjoying life while in their textile business and after it closed down. Their country band, The Travelers, featured my dad playing the piano and my mom as the lead singer. They were always the county's feature band at all the local bluegrass festivals. Sitting out in a field, freezing, on wet bales of hay was not at all my idea of fun. They also competed in talent shows. One show in particular featured a local talent, a band of two brothers, Ricky and Randy Traywick, one of which became known as the country star, Randy Travis. While playing in their band was a fun pastime for my parents, I would soon realize that it would lead me to my exit strategy out of this town.

I graduated high school a year early, and "knowing it all," I couldn't wait to leave this small town for bigger and better things as soon as possible. The opportunity presented itself through my years of listening and watching my parents perform. They met a couple who were also musicians that played in a large country and western club in Charlotte. They became close friends, and the couple soon had a newborn daughter that my parents simply adored, so we visited often. With a newborn child, this couple wanted less time on stage and more time with family. To make it happen, they relocated to Knoxville. During a visit to Knoxville the summer heading in to my senior year in high school, I also visited the campus of the University of Tennessee. At that moment of walking on that campus, a dream of going there captivated me. I had no idea how it could or would come true. I just knew I wanted to attend college there.

Then the couple had a great idea. I could live with them and be their nanny, use their address for in-state tuition, and with best-laid plans, I jumped at the chance to move to Knoxville, Tennessee, on June 3, 1979, seven days after I finished high school.

I was leaving to attend college! I was going to chase my dreams. It was really happening!

LESSONS TO SOAR

Take nothing for granted. What you have today could change in the blink of an eye. Be grateful always.

Grow through what you go through. Thriving through difficulties builds character, strength, and your faith. Growth allows you to hold your head up high, knowing you will get to the other side stronger, wiser, and more resilient.

Be independent, and smart about it. A high level of independence can be both good and bad. There are times when you need to depend on others to help you.

*"Look adversity
in the face and see it
as an opportunity
to learn, grow
and succeed."*

CHAPTER 2

BROKE, NOT BROKEN

When my exit strategy out of "Marshvegas" was confirmed, I visited Knoxville while still in my senior year of high school. During one of my first visits, I met the couple's cousin, and we began dating. We fell in love and planned to be married, and I would start getting my college degree shortly after the wedding.

Well, it didn't work out at all as I had hoped—the marriage or the college degree. Though he might have meant it at the time, the opportunity for college was never considered after we said "I do." My desire to work and go to college would ultimately lead to the divorce. He wanted a housewife that had his food on the table every night at 5:00 p.m. Working in the home was what he wanted from me, and it was more demanding than any job—and also lonely. I missed being around people. I learned very quickly that I wasn't going to be a partner, but a wife who was told what to do and when to do it.

Divorced and Homeless

At twenty years old, I found myself divorced, sleeping on couches, and showering at various friends' houses with my clothes in the trunk of my car. That car and those clothes were all I owned. I had a job and a small sum I was awarded in the divorce, which would get me my first apartment. I figured I only needed three months to get it all together. With the money from the divorce, my salary, and hopefully a little overtime, I could have my first and last month's rent to move into a one-bedroom apartment. I had done my research and though they were old, renovated barracks, the apartment was safe. The best part? I would again have my independence back and living on my own terms.

Working in a regional bank in Oak Ridge, Tennessee, for a little more than a year, I knew it wasn't the path for me. All the senior management were male, and every lady with tenure urged me to look elsewhere. They also knew it wasn't the place for me. I was hired at minimum wage, and they were barely making more than I was.

When Opportunity Knocks

The opportunity that would set the course for my next thirty-five years walked in the bank's door, in the form of a husband-and-wife team who were forming a new company. They owned a machine shop and were opening an industrial supply company. I had the pleasure of working with the husband for most of that year as one of my first clients, and he asked if I would be interested in leaving the bank to come work for them. Of course, I said yes, and he gave me the address and the contact's name. I set up the appointment for the following day at lunch. I was so nervous, but I needed something I enjoyed and that paid more than minimum wage.

The next day, I walked through an open bay door that led directly into the warehouse. It was a ten-thousand-square-foot metal building in an industrial park, packed with machine shops and competing companies to obtain business from various government contracts. There is where I met Mr. Jack Jones. They had brought Jack out of retirement to manage their new venture. I would soon learn why they wanted him for the job.

I first noticed his shirt needed ironing and his coffee mug looked like it had not been washed in a decade. However, through his gruff exterior, he had a smile and laugh that made his face and eyes very kind, and I felt at ease speaking with him. As I looked around his makeshift office with his messy, dusty desk, I knew I was about to leave the glamorous high-rise, with its suits, ties, and high-end furnishings and was entering a different world entirely—a metal building with grease spots on the floor and the smell of propane from the forklift truck.

The owner had asked Jack to consider me for the accounting position, but as we chatted, Jack quickly realized that I was not interested in applying for an accounting role. Jack apologized and explained that accounting was the more typical job for a female and my working in a bank led to the misunderstanding. My heart sank. The bank was not my cup of tea at all. Nor was accounting.

Thankfully, Jack saw the disappointment on my face as I stood and extended my hand to thank him for his time. As I was heading for the door, he asked, "What does interest you?"

I explained how I loved working in customer service, and that was how I had gotten to know the owner so well. I shared how my willingness to be a team player led me to the teller line after a massive employee walkout. Working with people and helping them achieve their goals and meet their needs was very satisfying to me. Since being hired, I had won multiple statewide bank awards for new accounts and money markets being opened. This caught his attention.

Listening, he said it sounded like sales and customer service was more what I had in mind and asked, "How would you like to be one of the first women in outside industrial sales?"

I'm sure he saw the fear in my eyes. He shared that if I accepted the challenge, he will teach me all the product knowledge I would ever need. He thought I would see doors open and that the opportunities would come. However, the biggest key, he said, was having a service nature, a competitive spirit, and a passion for winning.

What a day of excitement that was for me! I left there feeling optimistic and thought this was an opportunity like no other. I received a call the following day that I had the job if I wanted to come on board immediately. I explained I felt it necessary to turn in a two-week notice with the bank. Later that day, I spoke with my bank manager to learn that employees leaving the bank in lower management positions were not allowed to work a notice, so I took a long weekend and began my new position the following Monday at Express Tooling Company.

I learned quickly that you don't just start selling; you must serve first. In my case, I would serve in a small dingy warehouse behind a counter to wait on customers.

I was also responsible for documenting the inventory. There were shelving units lined with all types of products and an extensive inventory card system that I would use to log materials in and out of the warehouse. My primary responsibilities were meeting new customers, putting away incoming material, and answering the phones. This later led to me taking incoming calls in a customer service role, which I loved.

As I worked the city counter and started meeting customers—all men—face-to-face from various walks of life, I knew early on I was in for a challenge.

The counter was covered in stickers and posters that were eye-opening, to say the least. What I mean is that the first thing the customers would see when they walked through the door was me standing amidst a barrage of sexist and demeaning posters of women wearing bikinis or even less plastered to the front of the counter area and displayed on the walls behind me.

The other challenge I faced was not being able to assist the customer without Jack's help and knowledge. One of the major product lines was cutting tools. This included products such as drill bits, reamers, taps, and dies, which were foreign to me. Jack saw my frustration and even embarrassment from time to time and came to me with a great idea. The owners of this supply house also owned a machine shop across the street. Every day at lunch, Jack and I would go into the shop and watch the machines run using these various tools. From those visits, I could soon begin answering specific questions about the products in a way that took me from a "girl" behind the counter to a knowledgeable salesperson they could respect. The opportunity to roll up my sleeves and get in on the ground floor of how it all worked was invaluable and made a lasting impression.

Red Pens Leave Marks

An industrial supply house has many different products and provides the opportunity to sell unique material and items that we do not even carry in our distribution facility. From parts to equipment, I was learning about a lot of different things. One of my funniest stories was when I first called on Boeing. I was there to sell a very expensive overhead crane. I remember how nervous I was, and one of my worst habits, and still is, was chewing on pens. That particular day, I had a red pen. A few minutes before the gentleman came to greet me, I looked down, and my hands were covered in red ink. I immediately thought, "Oh my God, it's got to be all over my mouth!" I only had enough time to imagine that I must look like Dracula.

I was about to tell the receptionist that something came up when the person I was supposed to meet came out into the lobby. I decided I would put my hands behind my back, which meant I could not shake his hand, and hopefully, I would be able to tell by the look on his face whether he would be scared out of his mind. The good news? I had avoided getting ink on my face, but he looked at me weird when I would not extend my hand to shake his.

It might surprise you to know that we got the order and had a grand celebration. I was surprised too. How did I get the order? I called and asked for a second meeting, and while it was difficult and embarrassing, I explained what happened and why I acted so strange. He laughed with me, said that explained a lot and that he appreciated my candor. He said, that with that kind of honesty, I deserved the order. After some slight negotiation about the delivery schedule, I left his office with the purchase order.

I decided then and there I would be true to who I am. People want to do business with real people, not just the company that employs them. Companies come and go, but honest relationships last a lifetime.

I swore I would never chew on pens again, but that didn't last because I still do when I'm nervous or bored. It has its benefits, though. I always get my pens back when I leave them lying around.

First Female in Industrial Sales

Even though Express Tooling Company was owned by a husband and wife, the only time I ever saw the wife was when I worked at the bank prior to becoming employed. They put the business in her name as 51 percent owner, which qualified them to be a small woman-owned business enterprise. At the time, I didn't completely understand the implications or the full advantages. All I knew was that the benefits were huge because it helped them do business with companies like Martin Marietta, Boeing, and government agencies with many locations in the area.

The industrial field may not have been the career path I dreamed of working in, but it was rewarding and fun, and it led me to be one of the first female industrial supply salespeople. Back when I first got into this line of work, people didn't know what to call me. I was called a saleswoman or even a salesgirl.

I was competitive and wouldn't take "no" for an answer. While a man doing what I did would be considered assertive and confident, I would be called a "know-it-all b-tch." This only fueled the fire in me to prove I could and would be victorious. They would soon know what to call me—a successful force to be reckoned with.

LESSONS TO SOAR

When a door opens, pay attention. Sometimes the door opening is someone walking through it and heading toward you. Be open and curious.

Honesty really is the best policy. Especially when things don't go as you intended, owning up to it through your honesty will earn you respect and trust.

Speak up and know what you don't want. If what is being proposed isn't what you had in mind, speak up and you'll be that much closer to what you do want.

Being the first has its responsibility. It really isn't about being the first, but about how you are paving the way for others.

1

LEADING THE EAGLE WAY

With an eagle's eye view, prey can be spotted from nearly two miles away with a 340-degree panoramic field of vision. Their keen eyesight allows them to see in vivid color, even in varying shades. A leader must be a visionary to see opportunities ahead and from differing perspectives with clarity and focus.

"Having a one-track mind is OK, as long as your mind is on the right track."

CHAPTER 3

IT'S A MAN'S WORLD

Until mid-1990, you did not have to have an appointment to see a customer. It was a time that I loved because it was invigorating to see all the men sitting in the lobby and wondering what I sold. I learned early on that I did better if the person in the purchasing position was not a woman. Yes, you read that right. These were very different times. There seemed to be more jealousy and intimidation than the willingness to help other women grow. The famous quote by Madeleine Albright says it all, "There is a special place in hell for women who don't help other women."

Empty Promises

As the company grew, I became more successful in acquiring customers and larger orders. Because of my success, I spoke with my manager about a raise and finally giving me benefits. At that time, I was using my own car and was not getting any sort of stipend or reimbursement for its use or wear and tear. The owner did not know my circumstances and suggested that my financial situation should not be a concern because he assumed I had a husband to depend on. Really? Yes, really. And I wondered how many women just allowed this to be stated without fighting back. I fought back.

The success he was enjoying had nothing to do with me having a husband, I told him. I didn't have a husband, for starters, and even if I had one, it should be about the value I brought to the table for the company. After standing up for myself, I was made promises. Around that same time, Jack bragged about me to one of our large fastener suppliers, and the manager for this company offered me a job as the second female outside salesperson in the history of their company. They offered me a company car, an expense account, $30,000 per year, plus a commission, which was a lot of money back then.

I told them I would think about it and let them know later that day. I called Jack from a pay phone and told him I needed to see him and the owner. They were both waiting for me when I arrived. I revisited what I had asked him for earlier and shared that I had an offer from another company. I explained I would like to stay a part of the team, but he said I was fired for even considering the other position.

I cleaned out my desk and left with a heavy heart. At that moment, I knew I would never forget what Jack taught me. However, I also knew it was time for me to move on.

When I called to tell the new company I would take the position, my hopes were dashed. The general manager who hired me told me his regional manager told him he could not hire a female because the last one they hired was more interested in getting a tan than selling. I stood there holding the pay phone receiver in disbelief. I had just been fired for accepting this position that was offered to me!

Well, that wasn't an option and he had to come up with another plan, I told him. I emphasized that his offer got me fired. He thought for a minute and decided to go against corporate because he could increase his sales branch with me and get the promotion he wanted, which was his regional manager's job. The solution? My new boss hid my gender. For record keeping purposes, I became C. R. Johnson of Territory #3. I was told I could not attend any corporate functions for eighteen months.

Fasteners carry different meanings for different people. When I was first making sales calls, I would say I sold fasteners. Many of the plants were manufacturing products that had some sort of sewing department. I was a woman, so the receptionist automatically assumed I was selling buttons, pins, and zippers. When I would say, "No, I'm selling things like stainless steel screws and rivets," they would have a weird look on their faces and call the purchasing agent that bought their hardware requesting he come to the lobby. It was always a process, simply because I was a woman. I had to find another way to describe what I sold because screws would not work for the long haul. A specific incident only solidified this to be even truer.

One Friday, I went to work, and they gave me a T-shirt to wear on Monday for their twenty-fifth year in business. It read across the front in large letters, "BEST SCREW IN TOWN." Their logo was in the upper-right-hand corner, so in their eyes it was only an advertisement. I stood there looking back and forth at them and then at the shirt. I turned around and left my manager holding the shirt in his hand. No, I didn't wear it, though I eventually took one of those T-shirts and kept it as a reminder to never let them see you sweat. And I still have it to show today. From that day forward, I began saying I sold nuts, bolts, and screws. That served me well through the years.

A mere eleven months after I had been hired at the fastener company, I attended that corporate function because my territory had the highest sales, with the best profit margin in the eastern region. You should've seen everyone's mouths drop when I stood up for my award, and when they saw I was a woman! It was priceless! The manager still took all the credit because he 'trained me so well.' And he got his promotion to regional manager.

When his replacement came on board, he split my territory three times to prohibit my commission and base salary from surpassing his own. This would force me to scramble to obtain new potential customers each time.

"You Guys Make Me Nervous"

Frustrated, I saw a clear path for the opportunity to launch my own fastener business with the help of a single statement from my boss at a local trade show. As the show was winding down on the last day, I was walking the show and couldn't help but stop and check out my competitors' display areas. As I stopped by one booth to introduce myself, I found two different local distributors standing there talking. They had both worked together previously at my current employer's and were friends. I quickly learned they had a great disdain for the way their companies did business, just like me.

It also surprised me that they already knew who I was. They had been scoping out our booth to see their newest competitor. As we talked about how the local economy was booming with new factories and they had heard how I had made strides into one of the largest in the area, we looked up and saw my boss headed in our direction. As he walked by and said hello, he said, "You guys make me nervous. You may be talking about establishing your own fastener company." As my boss walked on by, we looked at each other and it was as if you could see the light bulb over our heads as our eyes lit up and I said, "That's a great idea!"

Boat manufacturing was making large strides for us in our company's sales. There seemed to be new manufacturers popping up weekly because the lakes of East Tennessee were a major attraction. I was gaining knowledge from the smaller builders and, after multiple attempts, I made substantial headway. I earned the company's status to be the backup supplier for a manufacturer that would become one of the largest boating manufacturers in the world. This also opened up a whole new world with an uncommon fastener material that would become a scorching commodity. This new offering would be more expensive than the commonly known fastener material and was not yet stocked in many warehouses across the country.

I went to the VP of Purchasing at this company and asked him what it would take to become their chosen fastener supplier. He shared some of his thoughts of what they would need immediately and the direction he saw the industry going. I had always believed in asking for the order, and I said, "If I can make this happen, can I have your business?" He said, "If you can make it happen, I will give you the opportunity."

I took the information back to my boss that same day. I explained to him this boat manufacturer's current supplier was in Phoenix, Arizona, and was having trouble supplying the product promptly. I explained if we would put it in our inventory, we could move into the first position, and that the company would become our largest customer. Excited and thinking this was a no-brainer, I was shocked by a we-don't-do-it-that-way mentality. In other words, we do not want to take a risk on a change, no matter the growth opportunity. He recited their current business model to continue to use multiple distribution locations, as has always been done. Basically, wait until the order comes in and then transfer the product to their designated destination. That meant with all the red tape, even though we were only fifteen miles away, we could deliver no quicker than the manufacturer's current supplier in Phoenix, Arizona, which was approximately two thousand miles away!

It was in that moment that I thought to myself, "If you won't do it, I will." There was a reason I had met those experienced guys at the trade show, and we had continued our conversations since that fateful meeting. I felt I could form a partnership to drive this opportunity home! The male-dominated industries' mentality left me thinking there has got to be a better way to run a sustainable, successful business while maintaining loyal and vested employees and customers.

I made my decision. And there was no stopping me. My dream to own my own business was going to become a reality as soon as I gave my notice and walked out that door. I marched into my boss's office determined and with conviction.

LESSONS TO SOAR

Help other women succeed. It's competitive enough without making everyone your competition. By helping other women succeed, especially in a male-dominated industry, you are helping us all succeed.

Know your worth. Knowing the value you provide puts you in a stronger position to ask for and get what you're truly worth and the ability to walk away from anyone who doesn't value you.

Focus on the goal, not the accolades. When being recognized is not the focus, then you can put your entire focus on achieving the goal. Reach the goal; earn the accolades.

“When facing the impossible, don’t be afraid, be inspired.”

CHAPTER 4

COUNTDOWN TO LIFTOFF

After officially giving my boss notice, he looked at me without blinking an eye and said, "You do realize you have a noncompete, don't you?"

I had been so caught up in dreaming. This was an important piece that I had indeed forgotten. How could I have forgotten something so important? Once again, I had just quit my job only to learn that what I had planned to do wasn't as I had thought it would be. Now what the heck was I going to do? I knew I could find a job. But according to my contract, I had to be out of the state of Tennessee, my territory, for a minimum of twelve months.

I contacted my future partners and told them what had happened. They were still with their current employers, and the fact we were planning to establish a company together was highly confidential. The plan was for me to get it going, and then they would come on board once we had a little cash flow to pay their salaries.

My mind was racing. This wasn't part of the plan. I—we—would have to wait a whole year. It didn't feel fair, yet it was totally legal and our reality. I knew I had to get a job quickly. My mind was racing with all my potential scenarios. I was a waitress when I was in high school and I could do that again. And then there was the bank. I decided I could make more as a waitress. I just knew I had to find a job immediately. Then I thought if I stayed in the industrial fastener field, I could continue to gain knowledge and grow a new potential customer base that I could poach later. As I write that word "poach," it sounds ruthless, but all is fair when a girl's gotta eat. Right?

Back to the Carolinas

At that time, my grandmother and aunt both lived in Greenville, South Carolina. I went to visit and told them of my dilemma. My aunt happened to notice that a fastener company in Greenville was hiring in sales. This could be perfect. It was only two hours back to Knoxville and around three hours to see my parents in Marshville, which made them very happy. I had to get this job. It would allow me to build a customer base I could later service from Knoxville, while continuing to learn the business. Most crucial, I could travel back and forth on the weekend to keep my dream moving forward.

I got the job in an outside sales position. I felt I was back on track. I had family close by and was very thankful for the opportunity to continue to grow both personally and professionally. I began making sales calls in my new territory and quickly realized the customer base differed greatly from Knoxville, which allowed me to learn about varying products and preferences.

The owner of this company, Max, was also the owner of a fastener manufacturer in Columbia, South Carolina. This meant I needed to learn about an additional segment of products and another industry as well. Not only did they manufacture products, but they coated the nuts and bolts with various rust inhibitors. Yes, they made nuts and bolts, not fasteners or the smaller screws and component parts that I was familiar with. They made very large bolts used in the construction industry—from holding up the foundation to a variety of other products. Not only was this a new market and product line, it was a new customer base that was not accustomed to working with women. I was still very much in a man's world.

With two fastener locations, one for the distribution of production components and the other focused on manufacturing and plating, I worked primarily out of the Greenville distribution facility. I enjoyed building a new client base, learning new products, and spending time with my family. My territory was much smaller than it had been in Knoxville, so I spent a lot less time in my car.

Standing My Ground

One of my core responsibilities was to work trade shows. Most people hate trade shows or they see them as goof-off time, but I always found a way to make them fun and productive. I made it feel like a fairground game, going out into the aisle to bring people into the booth. I figured if I was going to be there with my feet hurting, I might as well make it a success. Over the years, I've met many long-term customers at trade shows and wanted to continue that winning streak.

One particular show I worked was not a success—at least initially. On the first day of the show, a woman walked into our company's booth wearing four-inch heels, very short shorts, fishnet stockings, and her boobs were thrust up to her chin. It was the company owner's solution to the booth getting attention. No, I am not exaggerating. I had seen models work trade shows before, but this was sexism at a whole new level.

The show was in Myrtle Beach, South Carolina, and many of those in attendance used it as an opportunity for a family vacation they could use as a business write-off. Many potential customers were walking through the event with their wives. One look at the lady in the booth, and the wives would drag them down the aisle as far away from our booth as possible. While the model was meant to draw in traffic, it was backfiring. The bigger problem was trying to win credibility as a qualified and knowledgeable salesperson while this woman was being exploited right beside me. By noon, I had enough and went to my boss, explained the issue I had with the spectacle and said, "While you think about how this is really going to work, I'll be at the hotel pool," and I and walked out.

As I walked away, I wondered if a lesson could be learned here. Respect is vital for success, but few were willing to offer it, which meant I had to earn it. This was a pivotal time for me. It taught me to stand up for myself and my right as a professional woman in business. I learned to respect myself and know my worth, and to make sure others respected me in the same manner through my actions and what I would tolerate and not tolerate.

I didn't know if I would have a job after taking my stand, so why not go soak up some sun at the hotel? After all, I had paid for the room with the company credit card, and I decided I'd better enjoy the perk of an expense account while I still had one.

I don't know which was better, the sun, or the news the other salespeople brought back to me from the show that evening. As I had predicted, the scantily clad model didn't increase traffic. They had received hardly any visitors, with only two leads all day. I didn't lose my job. I was allowed to take charge. The next day, I showed him what a successful show looked like.

Having a Tough Skin

A few weeks later, I was back in Greenville and making calls. I had been blessed with a new contract that week and stopped by the office for a manager's signature. Everyone was standing outside as I pulled up. I got out of my car, and then I saw the problem. There were federal agents putting padlocks on the door and the owner was in handcuffs for tax evasion.

The rest of that day was a blur. I had no idea what this meant for me or anybody else. I wasn't even sure if the owner was going to jail. Then I watched the federal agents remove the handcuffs from Max and give strict orders for everyone to vacate the premises. As I stood there, I knew I was working for a crazy man. He was willing to risk jail time! I watched him break the padlocks and begin loading up large trucks with material to deliver to his other location. No way was I having any part of this, and as I was leaving, he came to my car window and asked me to give him a few days to work something out.

I was terrified on so many different levels. What do I do now? This job was salary plus commission. I was still building my territory, and I had little savings to depend upon. I was still five months away from being able to go back into the Knoxville area. Again, I was thinking, waitress, banking, another fastener company in another town? I decided for the next few days I would wait and pray.

On Tuesday of the following week, I got a phone call from Max. Would I work for his other location? I could still live in Greenville and commute to Columbia once a week, which was about an hour away. The additional time I would spend selling.

His other location was the division that manufactured bolts for the commercial construction industry. Purchasing was done right on the construction job site that was usually located in the center of the construction project for easy access to the personnel. This also exposed me to the less than gentlemanly workers in hard hats. They may have been there to make an honest living; however, they didn't mind having a little fun at my expense all at the same time. I was tormented and ridiculed by their catcalls, whistles, and profanity. Despite their behavior, I was unwavering in my determination to be a part of this world. I deserved to be there as much as they did and would hold my head high in the face of their sneers.

The posters and language on job sites were more than enough to remind me of the value of Jack's mentoring. One particular day stood out when I was still working with Jack that helped remind me I had what it would take to succeed. I had been making sales calls, and it had been a tough day. I had tears in my eyes when I entered his office. He looked at me sternly and said, "If you are going to make it in this industry, you will need to have a tough skin."

"What does that mean?" I asked.

"You must not let their distasteful remarks make you back down from who you are and the wisdom you bring to the table."

I knew I was purposely leading the way for other women in this predominately male industry, while also leading myself to great heights of accomplishment. From that point forward, my focus was on possessing a tenacious commitment to earn their respect through being laser focused. My number one priority was concentrating on my abilities, developing product knowledge, and presenting a totally professional image. I revisited that day with Jack many times to remind myself of the importance of my resolve. Respecting myself first and that, in turn, would provide me with more opportunities to succeed in their environment. Best of all, it started building my self-esteem and confidence. That is what really having a "tough skin" is all about.

Money I May Never See

Everyone was on edge since the incident with the padlocked doors in Greenville. There was never a dull moment from that point forward. For example, on my first trip to the manufacturing facility, I saw a vendor trying to take Max's huge diamond ring off of his finger for payment on past due invoices. I knew the end was near, but I still had three months before I could go back to Knoxville.

Around the same time, a few coworkers called me with the news that their paychecks were bouncing and they were inquiring about mine. Quickly, I called my bank, and my checks had all cleared. I knew it was only a matter of time. With the contract I had been awarded a short time prior and a new job site at my back door worth millions, I knew I was putting money in Max's pocket that I may never see, and it was time to negotiate my exit.

I called Max and told him about my plan to form a fastener company in Tennessee in a few months, and that I needed him and believed he needed me to make our plan successful. This man was crazy and volatile, but I was willing to take a gamble with his greed. Money ruled his life, and I believed he would say yes.

My gamble paid off. We agreed that once I left, I would stay away from two of his customers, and in return, he would send my payroll and expenses to me, in cashier's checks or cash, for the next three months.

That day, I was the big winner. The noncompete agreement with two customers was in my favor because with what I was seeing, Max would not be around for long, so they would be fair game. I had another customer I was developing that was bigger than those two combined, and I felt I could eventually close this deal for our new company in Knoxville.

By the end of the following month, I was becoming even more uneasy with the way Max was conducting business. I was getting my salary and my commission checks were clearing the bank, unlike other employees. What I was witnessing in the business world was downright frightening and wrong. I wondered if I had what it would take. As I traveled from jobsite to jobsite, and the time grew closer for me to launch my own company, I found myself losing my courage and the fortitude I needed to continue working for this company, but for now I would push myself forward.

I hadn't been able to save as planned. There had been too many barriers to getting the material to my customers, which led to declining commission checks. My dream felt like it was fading, and I was spending too much time in "what if land." What if I couldn't get it off the ground? What if no one took me seriously? What if it was only a pipe dream? What if, what if, what if? "What if land" has no zip code, but there are certainly different areas in which to reside. I realized I was living on the negative side in the way I was thinking, and my mindset had to change if I was going to make this dream of owning my own company a reality.

I decided it was time to do something about my future or fail from not having the courage to even start. It was time to leave "what if land" behind by focusing on the positive and what I had the power to do. I organized a list of things I could do prior to actually moving back to Knoxville and began checking things off.

I scheduled all of my calls in the Greenville and Columbia area in four days during the work week so I could spend long weekends in Knoxville with friends to lay more groundwork for the new business. The building that I found was three thousand square feet and had a lease of $500.00 a month. I knew someone who knew someone, and it would be available when we needed it, with only a twelve-month lease and no deposit. It was in a strip center beside a laundromat with no loading dock. Not having a loading dock would make it tedious to unload and load material, but you get what you pay for, and we would have to make it work. I saw this as a gift from God, that I was one step closer to making the dream a reality.

LESSONS TO SOAR

Stand your ground. If you believe something isn't right, don't be afraid to take a stand backed up by your reasons why. It will either earn you respect or confirm your next best step away from the situation. Either way, you win.

Know your audience and their leverage. Be aware of who may influence actions or decisions, not just who you assume is making the decisions.

Be open to what feels uncomfortable. What is uncomfortable now could be what makes things easier for you and others in the future.

"Being a one-woman show will only get you so far."

CHAPTER 5

DREAM IN MOTION

My partners and I thought of names for this dream we had. After a few weeks of discussions, we chose what we thought would be perfect. The name of the company became Victory Bolt, Inc. What better way to show a winning attitude than to use the name "Victory"?

We needed an image as strong as the name, and our logo was born—an eagle with a massive wingspan soaring through the air carrying our products in its powerful talons. As the years rolled on, the name and logo would prove to mean even more to me as a symbol of strength, courage, and focused commitment.

My partners, Jerry and Charlie, and I were from very different backgrounds, but equally brought great passion to succeed as entrepreneurs. From a business perspective, we each came from companies of various sizes that specialized in different product lines. Therefore, we, could bring a wide variety of customer and vendor types into the fold. While my specialty was customers producing high-volume items, Charlie's was smaller fasteners and component parts used in the electrical industry, and Jerry had a maintenance-fastener and government-procurement background. Our combined knowledge of all these types of fasteners would allow our potential customers to consolidate purchases, reduce their number of vendors, and obtain better service on many items rather than a few types.

We decided on the shares based on mostly experience. Jerry had an American Indian bloodline and would qualify as a minority along with all its benefits as long as he had a 51 percent share. He was also bringing the most experience and the most substantial vendor relationships. I was the one that had the experience in sales, and I had the start-up funding, a whopping $3000.00 and a credit card with a $10,000 credit limit at 21 percent interest. Based on this, I would take

36 percent of the shares, which left Charlie, our minority partner, with the balance of the shares. It was time to make it legal. The legal documents were created, signed, and filed with the state of Tennessee.

It almost seemed too good to be true. We signed the very inexpensive lease on our tiny warehouse, and it was actually happening. When we moved into our location, we discovered the building's entire wall was covered with asbestos. As I said, they say you get what you pay for. We removed the asbestos and carried on and thankfully, no one got sick.

A Misty Goodbye

Through this excitement, I was still working for the company in South Carolina. It was in my best interest not to drop the ball there. However, the service level that I was able to provide was waning more and more every day. We were becoming unable to meet our customer's delivery requests because of vendors not being paid and our manufacturing employees were leaving the company in droves.

I knew as long as I stayed present to work through these issues, the customers would say I have their best interest at heart. At this point, I was down to about thirty days until launch. I began planning my exit strategy, but I didn't anticipate what happened next. The decision to leave took a very unusual turn.

Amidst vendor and employee chaos, I had to make a sales call and a delivery to a job site. I got out of the car and headed to the metal building where they kept their construction material. As I was walking, I realized it was beginning to mist rain. I looked up and saw a man standing on scaffolding high in the air, urinating. That was the "mist" blowing on me. And that was it! I asked to use the phone in the receiving department and called Max. I told him I was done by the end of the week.

A few days later, I dropped off my company car, got a ride to the car dealership where I had bought a used car with one hundred thousand miles, and rented a U-Haul. My parents and a few friends from Marshville came to South Carolina and helped me load up. I gave my aunt and grandmother a hug and off I went to Knoxville.

Quitting sooner than planned had its repercussions. My apartment was not ready to move in yet. I contacted an old friend and she allowed me to stay with her for three weeks. The Victory Bolt location was where I kept my small amount of belongings. I spent the next three weeks setting up the books, phone system, finding used office furniture for our two office spaces, and doing a little decorating and sprucing up the place. I would make sure it didn't look dingy, grimy, and filthy, like the other industrial and fastener companies where I had been employed. The location of our new business was certainly nothing fancy and money was in very short supply, but my goal was to present a professional and respectful image in the best possible way with what we had to work with at that time.

Two Weeks Matters

It was grand opening time. Nothing fancy occurred. It just meant I went and unlocked the door and called on customers and vendors to get the ball rolling. It wasn't long before we started getting some orders. The orders were small, but I knew they would grow. I was steadfast in providing extreme customer service with a high level of gratitude. I knew with that approach to business our potential was unlimited.

With my partners still working for other companies, it was a one-woman show. I could hardly wait to get out of the car and see customers face-to-face. It was beginning to look like the other guys could quit their jobs and come on board sooner than expected, and that felt amazing. Then an official registered letter arrived from my former employer, Southeastern Bolt and Screw. It had grown to be one of the largest fastener companies in the country and owned by a conglomerate called Jim Walter Corporation.

The letter stated I was in breach of my noncompete. What? How could that be? I had been methodical in waiting to pull the trigger on Victory until I knew we were clear. What if it meant another twelve months of noncompete regardless of the violation time frame? How would I turn this adversity into an opportunity? I had no plan, and panic was setting in. I headed back to the depressed state of "what if land."

There was a difference of opinion when reading my noncompete contract. My attorney said it was twelve months from when I tendered my resignation. The corporate attorneys said it was twelve months from my last day of actual working, including the time I worked under notice. Regardless of who was right, this was going to cost money that we did not have. What next? Really? I had only missed the mark by two weeks, but still, if they won, it could mean another twelve months of noncompete being put in to play.

The word was out that I was back in town and had founded a new company. Also, there was gossip about who I was going into business with, and whether or not we were ready. My two partners now came on board.

When I met with our attorney, I was distraught, to say the least. I remember him looking at me with a smile and saying, "You should take this as a huge compliment. They are taking their time and resources to come after you. They must be concerned with what you are going to be able to do to their businesses."

I hadn't thought of it that way. Even so, what was I going to do?

The contract read that we would handle any dispute through mediation. On the day of the one and only meeting, I was shocked to see not one attorney but four attorneys present. Again, my attorney looked at me with a smile and reminded me they were scared. At that moment, I felt physically ill. Yes, it was intimidating. It was only later that I truly appreciated that moment we were in and the fact that my business and I actually intimidated them.

Subsequently, my attorney discussed this ludicrous idea of their suit and suggested that I offer to contact no customers for an additional three months. Their answer was, give us two weeks to consider this offer and we will be back in touch. We left there, and over lunch, he looked at me and said, "Get out of here and call as many new customers as you can until we hear back from them."

For those next two weeks, if the customer was in a sixty-mile radius and would be a top ten account contender, I was standing in their lobby asking to see the buyer. The majority I would have to call because time was so limited. I felt like I was chained to the phone. I was contacting and reaching customers that I had built relationships with through my other former employers. I needed the assistance of the vendors. It didn't matter how many customers came on board if we didn't have the material ready and waiting to support their needs. The vendors were more than happy to oblige because the companies I had worked for were either difficult to work with by demanding more than they deserved or did not pay their bills. I could start quoting competitive pricing to customers because our vendors were willing to give us the pricing we needed to be awarded the business.

I made it my mission to contact, build the relationships, and be competitive, yet not be the lowest bid. I kept my finger on the pulse of current pricing structures and service models while always looking for ways to soar above all of my competitors. I barely slept for those two weeks, making sales calls and phone calls during the day, and processing pricing estimates at night. My energy was endless, and I had to keep my thoughts about the lawsuit at bay. Selling my dream was the best way.

The end result is we won the mediation on our terms at the three months extended noncompete. The attorney also determined that the contract only stated that I would not contact any former customers, so my customers were indeed free to contact me with no fear of retribution. With that behind us, we could finally focus on our business. I do not know how to put into words how exhilarating this all felt. This was finally really happening.

I was thankful that I had not only survived this crazy time; I had grown both personally and professionally. I had stood up for myself, and I knew God had even better things in store for me.

LESSONS TO SOAR

Be your very best, especially amidst chaos. When everyone else is falling apart and abandoning ship, stay focused on how you can do your very best to serve, and you will come out ahead in ways you never imagined.

Walking away isn't quitting. Sometimes walking away is the only way to maintain your dignity, values, and focus.

Perfection won't get you there. Faith and perseverance, not perfection, are key to your success. Go with what you've got and learn along the way.

Always focus on what *you* can do. No matter what appears out of your control or out of your reach, there are ways around it.

"When confidence grows, so does conflict."

CHAPTER 6

I DO! I DON'T!

The three months that followed were a flurry of activity. Jumping in headfirst with very limited funding, our truck looked like it belonged to a dogcatcher, but it worked. It had some shelves in the back and magnetic signs for advertisement. We were good to go.

In those two weeks prior to our mediation agreement, I had promised I would be available by phone. Our potential customers knew about the noncompete and understood the dilemma I was facing. Them contacting me was essential to not being in breach of another noncompete. This meant my travel time had to be limited to slower call days, so I'd be available to answer their calls. From my days in Knoxville, I knew it would be on Fridays. I would line up a few appointments and would leave late on a Thursday evening. This limited schedule would allow time to stop at pay phones along the way to check my messages.

As I waited, not so patiently, for the phone to ring, I realized I didn't have a noncompete in upstate South Carolina. I could call and visit the customers who bought material within our product range and fit our business model. With the market segments being so different, there wasn't a lot of customer potential there. But when you're starting from scratch, every account counts and as we grew, so would our product mix.

I had learned from my earlier conversation with the large boat company that vendor-managed inventory would be the way of the future. I took his advice and created a program. Though very manual at first, it was successful. Showing customers I could provide them with superior service while cutting their purchasing costs and freight expenses with fewer and more complete weekly orders was new to the industry and was a hit. What this entailed was being turnkey—going into the plants and organizing their storage cabinets, taking the orders, delivering them in our new truck, putting the material away, and beginning the process again.

With this special service program in our arsenal, once I completed my contractual obligation with the noncompete, I could hit the ground running. It wasn't long before I couldn't keep up. Then we hired someone to do the accounting and payroll and someone to manage the inventory for the customers to free my time to obtain new business. We were growing in what seemed a controlled time frame, but that didn't last long.

Growing like Gangbusters

Within twelve months, we needed a larger facility. We went from two thousand square feet to fifteen thousand square feet and moved over a long weekend. Then we really saw the opportunities pouring in. That marine account I mentioned earlier awarded us their business, and it opened up our buying power tremendously. We were now doing business all over the Southeast. As anticipated, the marine industry was booming. We picked up a contract with a boat manufacturing company on unique parts in Miami, Florida. I was having a blast! Much of this didn't seem real. It was so far removed from a short time ago.

Jerry, the majority partner, and I quickly became great friends. I loved his work ethic. He was kind, had a great personality, and was very outgoing. We just had so much in common. We both worked so much, there wasn't much time to date. And the next thing I knew, we were more than just partners and friends. We were building something together personally, too, and enjoying every minute.

As the company grew, opportunities in my life grew as well. I could get out of the roach-infested, burned-out apartment complex I was living in, and was blessed with an opportunity to buy a lot and build my very own home. When applying for the loan, my salary had been too low the prior year, and because I was self-employed, there were no guarantees that my current salary would continue. I didn't take no for an answer and asked for other options, which led me to a special Department of Housing and Urban Development (HUD) financing opportunity as a first-time homebuyer at a low rate and no money down. I was ecstatic.

The house came along pretty quickly, and soon it was a reality. I had plenty of room and my parents visited often. Their life was going well too. Their financial health had returned, and they had adjusted to leaning on each other since I had been gone. We were closer than ever, and I loved sharing with them and getting their trusted advice. I was blessed to build a three-bedroom, two-bath, split-level home of about seventeen hundred square feet. I had an acre lot and I fenced it in for my fur babies—Sunshine, my blond cocker, and Ge-Ge, my black Shih Tzu. You could say it was nothing special. Except for me, it stood for greater independence.

Then, to my surprise, Jerry asked me to marry him. No date was set, but I was looking forward to our future. The company continued to thrive, and I was learning so much and grew in my confidence in business and negotiations. I loved making our outside sales, and because I was the primary one in front of the customers, I became the face of Victory Bolt, Inc. I felt like I was at the top of my game professionally and was also content personally.

A Pattern of Abuse

Over time, this altered as I saw changes in Jerry's personality, but didn't recognize the pattern of what was coming my way. The man who was wonderful in the beginning became physically abusive a few months after our engagement. He would devise reasons to go into jealous rages and kept track of my every move. At first, he would squeeze my arm in public as a show of control. Soon it was full-blown domestic violence—complete with doors being busted down to holes punched in sheetrock beside my head. When he would choke me, he would say it was my fault.

What made it worse was when Jerry realized I would not call the police in order to protect the reputation of Victory Bolt. He became out of control yet was still careful not to leave a visible bruise, carefully inflicting me where they were hidden by clothes.

One night it escalated to me running to the neighbors in my robe as he held a shotgun pointed at me. I thought the neighbors would help me. They kept me safe until he left, but at the time, where domestic violence was concerned, it was a private matter that should be handled behind closed doors. For me, it was personal and emotionally crippling. I was made to feel it was my fault. I was too ashamed to tell parents or friends. His family could have seen him strike me and would still say he didn't do it. My next-door neighbors saw the bruises around my neck and still turned a blind eye.

After each horrible night, he would shower me with apologies, romantic notes, and flowers, and he would swear it would never happen again. As I have learned since, that is what's known as the honeymoon phase that plays over and over again. When you are in this situation, you so deeply want to believe they will change, and I was no different. I think I knew the truth in my heart, but I also knew there was a different man in there, and I prayed he would come back.

Though I had tough times before, I had never experienced this physical pain with such an overwhelming mental toll. I was drowning in regret and dread. As I opened my eyes to a new day, I regretted who I had become. I was broken and needed to find a true source of guidance and strength. I found it in a large local church near my home in Knoxville. There I was baptized and began my long journey to finding out who I was created to be.

The first day that I took Jerry to church, the pastor looked at him as we were leaving the church and said, "So you are the evil in her life." I had never, ever, mentioned anything to anyone at church about what was going on in my life, so this was just further confirmation that I was about to do the only thing I could. I had come to love a verse that I had written in my sales notebook, and it was Genesis 50:20a: "You intended to harm me, but God intended it all for good."

I realized I was not only trying to help myself; I was trying to save Jerry as well. I had done what I could to change myself by bending backwards to be less confident. I was trying to fade into the shadows both professionally and personally. The key word here was trying. No matter what I did, it wasn't enough to change his poor choices in life or the situation. You can't change someone if they don't want to change. The worst part was his behavior was eroding my self-assurance and positive attitude. It was leaving me less effective and stressed beyond measure. I would learn later this is known as codependence, and I could have been the poster child.

The honeymoon phases would last for weeks and sometimes a few months, but never long enough. As in all relationships involving domestic violence, something will spark his temper or injure his ego and the cycle starts again. I realized nothing would change until I was ready to do something for myself, but I wasn't prepared. I was not giving up Victory Bolt, and I was literally in for a fight. At the time, I saw it as the fight of my life, and it was a fight I was going to win.

When Enough Is Enough

The morning came when I looked in the mirror after the most violent night of them all. It was in that moment, looking at my visible bruises, I said, "Enough!" That particular night, I called his brother, and he got Jerry out of my house around two in the morning. I got a little sleep and about ten that morning I got out of bed. My knee hurt so badly I could hardly walk on it, and then as I approached the mirror, I saw the evidence on my face. I saw it on my wrist, and I saw it on my neck. Bruises were everywhere. Right then, I knew it was not my fault. I couldn't and wouldn't change myself and that it wouldn't matter anyway. Later, I learned I had been experiencing the typical cycle of domestic violence, a cycle that would only continue to get worse.

I knew I was better than this, that he was the problem, and no matter what I did, I couldn't fix this situation and certainly not him. It was in that decisive moment that I saw a brightness come into my eyes that overshadowed the fog of depression that had been taking over me. I had learned that you cannot change those around you, but you can change those who surround you. For the first time in months, I could see clearly. I realized the stronger I was getting and the more independent I became, the more outraged he was. He was insecure and jealous of the woman I had become. Love shouldn't hurt ever! Rather than being a solid partner both personally and in the business, his goal was to make himself feel better by destroying me and my self-esteem. I would heal on the outside pretty quickly, but it would be a long road to heal on the inside. I would lose so much, but I was finally no longer stuck in it. I was determined to get through it, not as a victim, but as a victorious, strong, successful woman.

With this latest blow and carelessness on his part by leaving visible signs of abuse that all could see, I used the evidence on my body as a negotiating tool. I finally realized that as embarrassing as it may be, this was not my fault and he needed to take responsibility for his behavior and pay for what he had done to me and our company.

Using Pain for Gain

Later that morning, I put on a pair of sweatpants and a T-shirt and found an old cane that my grandfather had carved out of a tree trunk. I got in my car and headed to Victory Bolt's corporate attorney's office. I would use this pain and heartbreak to launch the next stage of my life.

The secretary stared at me in disbelief as she asked if I had an appointment. I'm sure she wanted to know what happened to me, but didn't dare ask. I looked at her as intently as I could and said, "I'll wait."

She knocked on his door and it was only a few minutes before he came out to see me. He looked at me and said, "What? Oh my God! What happened? Were you in a wreck?"

"No. Jerry did this, and we need to talk."

He took me into his office, and he asked me if I wanted to press charges. I told him from the research I had done that it would be futile, and I had another idea that would be better for everyone. Even the employees would keep their jobs and the customers and vendors would never know. This plan was for my safety and the future of the company.

Knowing me and my tenacity, the attorney said, "This should be interesting."

LESSONS TO SOAR

Do what you can where you can. When you stop focusing on what limits you, you start seeing a variety of options and directions in which to go.

Find the key to turnkey. Making it easier, more affordable, or more efficient for the one you are serving is the key to being their secret weapon toward success.

Don't stop until you know all your options. You will never know what may be the perfect solution if you don't ask or push to know all that is available for you to consider. Never accept "not possible" at face value.

Be you and no one else. Attempting to change who you are for someone else will only bring you crashing down. Lift yourself up by the strength of who you are and how you want to be.

"But she was given two wings like those of a great eagle so she could fly to the place prepared for her in the wilderness. There she would be cared for and protected from the dragon for a time, times, and half a time."

—Revelation 12:14

"Sometimes the answer is right in front of you."

CHAPTER 7

VICTORY IS MINE

On that day in Victory's corporate attorney's office, I told him I wanted to branch the business into Charlotte, North Carolina. The ownership would maintain the same percentages until the one in Charlotte had become just as profitable. Then at that point, I would give up my ownership in Victory Bolt in Knoxville and become sole owner of the location in Charlotte. The attorney asked, "What is your plan if he doesn't agree?"

I reminded him how I looked and that this time I took pictures. But more importantly, I was the backbone of the company as far as the customers were concerned. If he didn't agree, I would launch my own company next door and proceed to take every account I could. This was an eye-opener for the attorney, and it became abundantly clear that I was right. He said he would schedule an appointment for all of us to meet within the next few days. I also told him to call Jerry that day to tell him he had seen me, and that if he came near me again, I would obtain a restraining order, no matter the consequences it might have on the company.

Within a few days, we were moving forward with a branch in Charlotte and the bruises were healing. While negotiations were in process, I could walk better and cover the bruises with makeup. And then, amidst this chaos, a miracle happened, and I just knew the timing to move forward was a perfect blessing that had dropped right in front of me.

As soon as I felt up to it, my first call was to our largest customer. I was told that they were expanding and opening a new manufacturing facility. I had to ask twice where it was going to be located because I couldn't believe my ears. They were renovating a building in Fort Mill, South Carolina. It was going to be the size of their first location in Knoxville, with a similar production model. Based on the sales of this location, if I could become the supplier of their new location, I could support my branch with just this one account. The next great news? I had worked closely with the decision maker that was being relocated to the Fort Mill location. I got on the next plane to Charlotte.

Twenty-four hours later, I was standing in the new manufacturing facility that was being renovated from a textile plant into a boat manufacturing facility. It was expected to be operational within ninety days. The best thing about doing business during those days was the ability to shake someone's hand, look him or her in the eye, and know you had a deal. With my commitment to a local branch with enough inventory combined with our vendor-managed inventory program, I would be their sole fastener supplier.

Limitations Breed Opportunity

I flew back to Knoxville the following morning to complete the new branch negotiations with Jerry and the attorney, and they were mostly in my favor. They introduced a caveat that I could not go in to the state of Tennessee to build my branch with any current or potential Victory customers. That really was no surprise, and I didn't fight it. I knew that if things didn't change there, it would be a moot point in the near future. The location in Knoxville would not be around for me to worry about.

I obtained a reputable commercial real estate firm in the Charlotte area to find my location in Charlotte, and one that was a short drive to the new customer in Fort Mill. They found a reasonably priced three-thousand-square-foot facility on the south side of Charlotte in a small industrial park. The cost meant as much or more to me as the location, and this was one of the few options I had.

Leaving Knoxville, agreed-upon material was loaded on a small truck to Charlotte along with desks, office supplies, and one very experienced employee to answer my phones, take care of inside sales, and customer support. That left me with one big hole in my plan. I needed someone to work in the warehouse and make pickups and deliveries. I knew exactly the person to take on that role—my daddy.

My dad had worked in textiles most of his life and it was his first love. He was raised in a mill working on looms and inspecting cloth at a very young age. I approached him that night at dinner and his exact words were, "I'm too old to change now."

I looked at him and said, "Really? You are only fifty years old, and I need you. Like Jack had taught me, I will teach you the industry and you will make this opportunity even better. And I will have the confidence that you are there—someone I can really trust to watch over things when I'm on the road selling." A few days later, he was on board 110 percent, and I had a very small army to make this a reality.

Who You Know Matters

I had been in Charlotte for about four months, living with my parents until my house in Knoxville sold. On the business front, things were humming right along. I had set up the fastener area at my one customer's location and then the news came I had an offer on my house in Knoxville. After a little negotiation, the deal was signed and I could move forward with moving out of my parents' house, either with an apartment or hopefully, purchasing a new home. Even when my house sold, I still struggled to make it happen because houses were twice as expensive in Charlotte compared to Knoxville. Apartments were much more expensive as well.

Then, a work associate's realtor husband told me about a subdivision in Matthews, North Carolina, with quaint wooded lots and the opportunity to get a house for under market value because the builder had filed for bankruptcy. While not great for the homebuilder, it was good news for me. The house I chose was scheduled to be finished within sixty days. Since it was still under construction, I could choose many of the amenities inside the home that would reflect me and my new life.

Around the time the house was completed, my best friend from high school called, wanting me to meet her fiancé's roommate. I hadn't dated since I left Knoxville, and she knew this. I decided, what the heck! There's no harm in going to a cookout. On the way to the house, I had washed my car earlier in the day and had left the sunroof open. My entire backside was soaked. I stopped in the McDonalds and went into the bathroom. I locked the door, got up on the sink, turned my butt to the hand dryer, and pushed the button. It worked. I was late getting there, but I made it with dry pants. It wasn't long before I told April what had happened, and we all got a good laugh. My blind date thought it was hilarious too and said, "I was a little intimidated when April told me about you, but I see you are very down to earth and wholesome." A few months later, Robert and I were engaged to be married.

I was planning a wedding, moving into my new house, and fighting to become the sole owner of Victory Bolt II. Part of the negotiation for the branch was that the home office would manage the accounting for both locations. About four months into the branch being open, vendors and customers began contacting me. Vendors were not getting paid, and customers were not getting their material on time. They both were looking to me for help.

Seizing the Opportunity

One large customer was receiving deteriorating customer service and no product support. It was the location that built $2,000,000.00 yachts and this location also housed all the corporate decision makers. What made these phone calls even more intriguing was that it was the parent company to the boat factory that I was supplying in Fort Mill with no problems. I saw an opportunity to obtain it all, and I knew I had to put a plan together quickly. This was a use-it-or-lose-it opportunity. I had worked too hard to lose it and I was going to do everything possible to use it. This was my chance to swoop in and capture 100 percent of this customer's trust. And they contacted me, so I know another noncompete would not be an issue again.

My first move was hiring an attorney in Charlotte. He contacted the corporate attorney in Knoxville. He set up the meeting for the following day. This would mean sitting across the negotiating table from Jerry, and I hoped it would be for the last time. My attorney did the talking. I wanted to own the branch outright or I would be forced to go into full competition against them. Even though my branch had not grown to equal value, the Knoxville location was declining fast. I needed to make a move now rather than later.

My second move was I needed to forge even stronger relationships with the vendors that we currently represented. I not only needed their quality brands, I needed substantial credit limits. Many had reached out to me several times in an effort to collect on invoices from my parent company in Knoxville. They knew the pressure I was feeling because they were feeling it too and were not surprised by my phone call. As I discussed my plan to obtain full ownership of the location in Charlotte and get my former accounts to join me from East Tennessee, they had an idea of their own. Each one agreed they would allow us to be authorized distributors for their products if we could keep a similar name to Victory Bolt. Last, I negotiated to pay the past-due invoices for the material that had shipped to my location, if they would agree to an ample credit limit to keep us moving forward with room to grow. I wouldn't know until later how difficult this would be.

Leveraging Strong Relationships

With declining sales, Jerry had become desperate for cash, which meant I had to get this deal done before everything was gone. Within three short weeks, I owned my own company 100 percent, and Victory Bolt & Specialty, Inc. was born. But we did not finalize the agreement without a bit of a sting from my perspective. By the time the papers were signed, they had used my receivables to pay the debts in Knoxville, not the vendors owed in Charlotte, which left me with payables that were ninety days old and receivables that were thirty days old. With more going out than coming in, it would mean some intense renegotiations with the vendors. Fortunately, my strong relationships proved it was manageable. If they didn't play ball, they would have to deal with the write-off. They decided they were better off waiting a little while longer for the money than to forfeit it. We successfully negotiated it on both sides and quickly continued moving forward.

As part of the deal, I also obtained the inventory in my warehouse, which amounted to approximately $50,000 in value. This was not much in the big scheme of things, but would generate cash flow as I sold the inventory. I also got the "dogcatcher" company truck and that was about it.

Now I was safe, independent, and owned the company outright, just as I had envisioned. I had successfully maintained a similar name, Victory Bolt & Specialty, Inc., which meant so much on so many levels. For the business, it meant that by keeping a similar name, my customers didn't know that I was now standing on my own without the support of a parent company, and the vendors were satisfied with our little "charade" because I had earned their trust. For me, it meant just what the name says: Victory. I had won this battle. Of course, there would be more to come, many more, but with each one I learned valuable lessons that gave me opportunities to grow as a person and an entrepreneur.

LESSONS TO SOAR

Teach others what you know. In order to grow yourself, you need to be willing to help others grow through what you know. What they can then handle for you allows you to focus on your next big challenge.

Use it or lose it. When an opportunity presents itself, take action immediately, even if it is to learn more. Victory cannot be realized without taking action.

Relationships are your secret weapon. Nurturing relationships is about valuing them and showing it in all your interactions. When you do, these same relationships will step up for you in ways you could have never imagined.

2

LEADING THE EAGLE WAY

An eagle possesses unsurpassed hunting skills and isn't intimidated by the size of what it desires. Leading others requires facing our adversaries fearlessly, staying focused on the ultimate prize in the end no matter the battle we face.

"When the unexpected is greeted with gratitude, the world opens its arms to you."

CHAPTER 8

NEONATAL MIRACLE

I now could truly move forward personally and professionally. I got married on a cold February day and then we headed for sunny Aruba. When we got back, I had to focus full speed ahead on the business. When you are down one employee and only had three to begin with, it puts quite a strain on the two left behind. I was working sixteen-hour days and felt run-down. I was losing weight, and I thought that the vomiting was coming from my awful diet and nerves.

I made a doctor's appointment and after some bloodwork and a few other tests; the doctor came in with a smile. She said, "Congratulations! You're pregnant!" I remember crying as she handed me a tissue, only to then reach and hand me the whole box. (I was really crying.) I informed her, from a prior issue, that I had been told I couldn't have children and that my husband and I had decided we could adopt.

It was a surprise on so many fronts. As you can imagine, being pregnant was the furthest thing from my mind, especially since it wasn't something we thought was possible. I had a new company that I had almost given my life for, so how could I make this work?

As I reached my car, my mind was reeling with possible scenarios of utter failure on all fronts of my life. How would I juggle a new business, a new marriage, and a baby? With the business, I had a strong plan of action, and I felt a sense of competency from prior experience. Simply put, I was self-assured and confident. Having recently come out of a troubled and violent long-term relationship, I wasn't as confident in the marriage arena. I was still healing and working my way through trust issues. It seemed to be going well and growing stronger over time. But a baby? I had no idea how I would manage adding raising a child and being a good mother. This was too many plates spinning in the air. How would I keep them from crashing to the ground?

Tears of Joy

I started driving toward home, and it hit me. My goodness! I'm pregnant! Once again, the tears flowed, but this time I was saying thank you, thank you, thank you, Lord. I would make this work. I was going to have a baby. This was a small anniversary as well. We had been married six months to the day, and the doctor said I was probably about three months along. I headed to tell Robert the great news with an anniversary gift—baby booties.

It was a rough pregnancy with constant bladder infections and gestational diabetes. I was on antibiotics and a diabetic diet for most of the pregnancy. At seven months, you could hardly tell I was pregnant, but the heartbeat was good. The doctor said there was nothing to worry about and I kept working through the constant back pain.

One day, it was more than I could handle, and I stopped by for a quick doctor's visit before heading to my next appointment. I told him I had not had pain this bad before and he said it was just Braxton Hicks contractions and sent me on my way. I drove to my appointment in Rock Hill, South Carolina, about forty miles away. The next morning, I got up and saw blood on the sheets. I was in pre-term labor.

I was in the hospital for a week before I convinced them my water was leaking. They had me on all types of medication to stop the labor and repeatedly told me that the fluid I was feeling was probably urine leaking. Finally, they had a shift change, and my mom told this particular doctor if they didn't do something, I was going to die. My blood pressure was through the roof. I was swollen beyond recognition and the muscle relaxants I was taking to stop the contractions were keeping me from even walking to the bathroom on my own. He examined me and I told him again I thought my water was leaking, and he finally checked the fluid. I was right and about thirty minutes later; they came in pulling out all the IVs to transport me by ambulance to a larger hospital that had a neonatal intensive care unit (NICU). I was going to have a baby eight weeks early.

The labor was slow to start, and they eventually induced it after thirty-six hours of contractions without a lot of progress. She was born about six hours later and I barely got to see her before they whisked her to intensive care at three pounds, eight ounces.

Later that night, they came with a wheelchair to get me. I was all cleaned up and feeling better than I had in months. I was just eager to see my baby girl. The nurse looked at me and said we should hurry. My daughter was in distress; I asked if she would be OK and was told it would be touch and go for the next several days.

They lifted me from the chair to where I could see our tiny baby with tubes and wires running everywhere. The NICU was so bright and noisy, with monitors and machines beeping everywhere. It was the saddest place I had ever seen. They hooked her up to a monitor because they said her brain stem had not completely formed. To put it simply, she would forget to breathe. The machine would warn them if that happened, but the real concern was the machine wire coming loose.

The machine began beeping. I'm looking at Heather and she's not breathing. She was turning blue, and they went to work and within a few seconds, which seemed like hours, she was breathing again. They assured me she was in the best place possible, and it was time to go get some rest. I was allowed to stay another night in the hospital.

Leaving the following day without Heather was one of the hardest days of my life. She dropped to two pounds, six ounces before she turned the corner. She was showing signs of growth again, and they were taking her off oxygen from time to time because they were very encouraged. It was standard practice for a preemie to stay in the hospital until their actual due date, but not my girl. She was home in three weeks.

While Heather was still in the hospital, I could not stay in the infant intensive care unit. I spent my time working, and it kept my mind occupied. My business was closer to the hospital anyway, and I had a lot to do before she came home.

When she came home earlier than expected, I quickly became exhausted. We had to make sure Heather continued to gain weight, which meant feeding her around the clock every two hours. The hospital said she wasn't a candidate for the machine that monitored her breathing because for twenty-four hours before she came home, she hadn't had an episode. Not comfortable with their mere one-day logic, I was checking on her constantly out of fear she might have an episode. Her dad was there to help during the night, but was working for a local cable company during the day. Rather than sleep when she slept, I had to work during the day.

Costly Complications

It wasn't long until the hospital and doctor's bills were coming in. I had been told by my insurance agent that any complications for me or the baby would be covered, just not the actual delivery. I called the insurance carrier within the twenty-four-hour window after she was born to add her to the policy as a dependent. But the claims for my week in the hospital and all of her medical bills were being denied. I had medical insurance, but no maternity insurance, and the bills from the hospital were all being linked to the delivery. We were looking at bills of close to $50,000.00 and I was a basket case by this added stress on top of it all.

Being a new solo owner of the company, I had taken a major hit on my salary. I went from almost $50,000.00 per year, which was a lot of money back then, to $12,000.00 per year. I was willing to do anything to make this business successful and knew that this salary would only be for a short period of time, but to pay these unforeseen bills was quite the stretch.

I took everything from the office that I needed to work from home. When Heather slept, I worked and once again found myself exhausted. At the same time, I was feeling extremely blessed with our new little family. But when she was four weeks old, I had to get back to the office and to visiting customers.

Since I was the owner, I could do what I wanted, and I took Heather to the office with me. It was difficult, and I was thankful for her PawPaw who was there to help. We made it work for a while. I was building a business and needed to be face-to-face with customers and vendors. This was very difficult with a newborn and my dad had his own work to do. I had no choice but to consider other options for childcare.

Then the Lord sent us Julie. We posted an ad in the paper and a lady thought she recognized my husband's name and called. It is hard to believe that it was a coincidence, but they had a mutual friend from high school, and she was looking for a private nanny position. Julie came on board for three years at a very fair price and it was a match made in heaven.

LESSONS TO SOAR

Trust your intuition. Experts may know what they know; however, your inner compass also knows. If it doesn't feel right, you have the right to question it.

Embrace the miracle of life. We all come from such meager beginnings, brought into this world naked and totally dependent. Giving thanks begins with our first breath.

"There is divine potential in every choice you make."

CHAPTER 9

FURIOUSLY PADDLING

Juggling a marriage, baby, and business were wonderful and trying times, mostly on the business front. With business growth comes the fine balance of managing cash flow, and it wasn't long before we were having some cash flow issues and I had to deal with how to meet our payroll obligation. I still had the credit card from the days at the Knoxville location, and as part of the business separation deal, it had been paid off. Problem solved. I used that credit card for a cash advance to make payroll for four weeks. I did this without mentioning it to anyone. I couldn't let my inside salesperson and my dad, yes, my dad, know the distress we were in on the cash flow front. It was just part of being a business owner with your name and your assets on the line.

Thankfully, that cash flow crunch was short-lived. I had obtained a new account in Florida resulting from a customer referral. It was large enough that I bought champagne and we had a small celebration. I offered the customer a cash discount if they paid within ten days and that was an incentive enough for them to pay early. This strategy would pay off with the early payment they made and returned us to cash flow positive and headed back in the right direction.

It was around this time I became more intentional about sharing my inside business details with my customers. I figured the honesty and openness that had worked with the vendors could pay off with customers, too. I learned that when you really talk to people, if asked, they wanted to help, as long as it was beneficial to them. A win-win, so to speak. I worked to make them feel a part of my business, that they too would be successful, and receive optimal service and competitive pricing. I learned over time that this was the culture I would become known for. And I learned businessmen didn't tend to create this type of culture.

When I first opened the branch in Charlotte, I had presented myself to new potential customers as part of a larger company. As I became sole owner, I elected to keep that fact to myself even though it no longer rang true and hadn't for several months. By this time, however, I had done what I had promised. I had proven to be competitive, quality-minded, and had provided a level of service beyond what they had received previously.

It was time to share the details of precisely what they had been a part of by simply telling my story. I would share with an abundance of gratitude how they had been a part of making our partnership and growth sustainable. They too had become a successful part of a new female-owned company. And most importantly, we were dedicated to fight tooth and nail to overcome whatever came our way to keep making it a win-win.

As we continued to grow, our competitors tried to use me being solo and woman-owned against us, but they did not prevail. While a few of our accounts did not like the idea of a woman running her own company, overall, being true to who we were led to customers that would prove to be true partners with us.

The response to sharing Victory's history and what we offered became more positive each day. It led to organic growth within each customer facility, and their sister companies came on board as well. I also found that sharing the struggles with lessons learned gave them a positive outlook that also benefited them. Knowing the adversities we had overcome, they felt we could be forward thinking to solve issues for them as they arose.

Their letters of recommendation flowed, and customers were actually coming to us with opportunities for us to problem solve. As I continued to make sales calls and research the market, I learned that most of my competitors offered the bare minimums both in product types and services. Armed with this information, I re-designed my three-year business plan based on a diversified customer base, special fasteners, adding component parts, and adding a heavy concentration on my vendor-managed inventory program. Most of the companies in the area had been there for years and were complacent about how they did business.

At this point, our customer base was continuing to grow. One customer made mammogram machines that were brand new to the market and they were booming.

Bloody Mary Moment

The owner of that company would later steal from the company and leave me holding a large receivable that would not be paid, which left a large payable to vendors still outstanding. No one saw it coming. He paid his bills and the employees right up until the time he "took the money and ran." He had been taking their payroll deductions for insurance and their 401(k) and pocketing it. His vendors were left holding the bag on more than $1 million dollars. He only owed me $10,000, which I thought I could take care of, but when the vendors forced him into bankruptcy, I had to give back money he had paid me thirty days prior to him shutting the business down. Yes, that's right, that's a bankruptcy law. That made it $30,000.00 total. I recall calling my daddy and having him come and get me. It was a Bloody Mary afternoon. I would like to say that is not the way I handled it, but it's what happened.

The next day, I pulled myself up by the bootstraps and went to work. This issue would not fix itself and I would not let this crook stop me in my tracks. I said a prayer and picked up the phone. I took the honest approach and talked to my vendors about what had happened and, once again, they chose to work with me. Another potential catastrophe diverted and much to be thankful for in how building solid relationships is priceless when you need them the most.

Busting at the Seams

Despite these challenges, we continued growing and were running out of room. There was a need to hire another inside salesperson and warehouse person. I also realized that I had to spend some money to make some money and hire a part-time bookkeeper. I could make far more customer contacts if I could take this off my plate. The problem is, I had nowhere to put them. We were already crammed into the office area and were talking over each other when on our phones.

I had built a strong relationship with the company next door to me on the other side of the concrete wall. They were one of the first soft indoor playground manufacturers, the playgrounds like you see in McDonalds. Mr. Pentes, the owner, was one of the most creative and savvy people I had ever known. He and his wife had created a loyal team of employees totally dedicated to the company and their process. I wanted to create the same kind of culture as we continued to grow.

Mr. Pentes came over one day and said, "I just got another contract and I want you to supply my fasteners and cable ties, but where are you going to put the material? You are busting out at the seams."

His question was very timely, and I explained the landlord would not let me out of the balance of our lease or lease me another spot at a reasonable price with less than a three-year term. I explained I couldn't afford to buy myself out of it, and that I would figure it out. I told him I had found a location across town that was twice as big and almost the same price that I was paying. It was not in an industrial park, but would work very well. I remember saying the timing must just not be right.

Two days later, Mr. Pentes came into my office and asked me if the building across town was still for lease. I didn't know, so he asked me to find out and let him know. It was still available and when I went to him with the news, I will never forget the moment when he said, "Ruth and I have taken care of your lease problem, and you can move." It took me a minute to compose myself and then to ask, "What are you talking about?"

Mr. Pentes leveraged his clout and told the owner that he needed more space and asked that the wall be removed in between our industrial suites to create one. At first, the owner's answer was no, that the suite on the other side was vacant and available. But Mr. Pentes threatened not to renew his leases on seven other locations with this owner if he didn't cooperate.

Within two weeks, I had signed the new lease, and I began the relocation process to a twelve-thousand-square-foot building. This location had high ceilings so we could use shelving and a rack system to create three times as much space as my first location. As I look back and think of this time in my life and others, I know God puts people in our paths for reasons we may never understand. Not only did the man God put in my path help me launch my business in the playground industry, he allowed me to grow it faster than otherwise possible. I have learned over the years, many, many times, that God will make a way—no matter how big or small the need is—when it is in His timing.

Ramping Up Amidst Slowdown

These were exciting times, and I used the move as a marketing tool to say thank you to the customers for helping us grow. Now we could handle more business. Though we were growing, the economy as a whole was softening. While a softening market may seem to be a negative, I saw opportunity. That meant there were qualified people looking for jobs and material costs were at a lower market level than usual.

With margins greater than usual, I hired the people we needed, and this enabled me to make more calls and increase sales. I learned that when the market is soft, many companies are not as aggressive, thinking that when the market gets strong again, their business will too. But this is not the way to do it. While everyone else is slowing down, it is a prime opportunity to ramp up. I have always grown in a slowdown. The buyers have time to talk because they are not as busy. Because other suppliers aren't calling, they are more open to what you have to offer and to review pricing. This strategy is a great time to sneak up on your competitor and take their customer. When you "never let 'em see ya' coming," it makes it hard for them to recoup what they lost.

Our ramp-up amidst the slowdown was working and then something occurred that could have been a setback—the original customer that allowed me to move to Charlotte in Fort Mill had not survived and they had closed the plant. This would have been devastating, but we were entering the years of the Reagan economic period and the recession was short-lived, with the economy becoming very robust. We had established enough business from other customers to not only survive, but thrive.

We were making a mark on the industry, and we needed to continue to stay in front of our competitors and at least keep up with the big boys and show our customers we were here to stay and could offer them as much as any of their suppliers, no matter how big or small.

Before I knew it, we had put in racks and done all the capital changes to make the current warehouse space as efficient as possible. We had hired several new warehouse employees and had grown to need a full-time accounting person. We added our first computer system, which was a big deal—no more inventory cards and manual bookkeeping. As part of this program, we also needed to work toward a quality program for our products and vendors, which included lot and serial numbers from where the material and product was produced.

We needed a full-time quality manager and, against my better judgment, I hired my husband, Robert, to fill that position. He received the necessary training on the system and products. Our quality program began slowly and grew over time as we implemented the new computer tracking systems.

Our customer base had grown to be quite diverse, from very large boat manufacturers like Sea Ray to utility construction like Duke Power, to equipment manufacturers like Valmont, along with a variety of smaller users that would continue to diversify our customer base and balance out profits.

I learned that the larger the customer, the smaller the margin and vice versa. I also learned that special products brought larger margins to the table while we also needed the lower-margin common items to accommodate our customers' every need. This taught me we needed to develop our culture to be a mindset that size doesn't matter. Every customer is a potential great customer, and our goal is to develop a long-term relationship with each and every one.

The quote "Do what you say you are going to do, when you say you are going to do it" hung in the hallway for many years at my company. It was drilled into every Victory team member to make it clear that all of our customers were made to feel like they were the only one we had.

Denied Five Times

When funding the needs of a new business, I found that baby steps were the way to go. I moved as my cash flow allowed without creating debt, because up to this point, I had been surviving, as my grandmother would say, "on a wing and a prayer." I was forced to do it that way since I had been denied credit five times amidst my company's growth, because I was a woman.

I knew eventually that in order to achieve the growth I desired, I had to acquire a line of credit, and had been working on it for several months. I needed to find a bank that would understand the needs of a small woman-owned business. My company had gained enough customers to pay all our overhead plus making a small profit in under twelve months. Armed with financials and a three-year business plan, even after being turned down by five banks, I set out to find the bank that would listen.

The kicker to this is that I was only asking for a $5,000 line of credit. I had ample credit limits with all of my suppliers, most of my customers were paying on time or even taking discounts when offered, and my cash flow was positive. The main reason I needed to have a credit line was so that I could tell potential vendors there was one in place. I had heard that a bank would only lend you money when you really didn't need it. Knowing this, I thought it would be an easy ask. After all, it was only $5,000. What I soon realized was that it was about the right person to ask. It's not what you know, but who you know.

That's when my mother recommended a smaller bank and the banker who would make a tremendous impact on my business. John was a unique individual that worked for a bank that genuinely was interested in helping the community grow. My mom thought he would listen to my story and understand my needs. That day, I walked away with a $20,000 line of credit. I am eternally grateful for the opportunity he gave me.

It was shortly after gaining that line of credit that I was learning more about the opportunities afforded to women and minorities that held more than 51 percent of the ownership. Since I owned 100 percent, I moved more intentionally in this direction. One of my customers, Progress Energy, now a part of Duke Energy, said it was a must. As soon as I filled out the necessary paperwork, passed the site visit, and obtained a Women's Business Enterprise National Council (WBENC) certification, their business doubled with us.

They became a customer pivotal to the growth of my company. I learned more with them than any other customer at the time. They taught me how to work with their engineering groups for product development and approvals. I could list my company as a manufacturer on each product drawing. With each approval, this strategy helped grow market share without ever quoting a price. For me, it would prove to be one of the most valuable techniques that I ever learned to put into play.

LESSONS TO SOAR

Getting ahead means thinking ahead. While you may not have all the answers, you always have options. Be open to multiple ways to get what you need to accomplish done.

Share your story with others in mind. It is only through acknowledging, and engaging with others that your story has wings. It then becomes a story they want to be a part of.

Problem solving takes forward thinking. Don't concentrate on the problem. You already know the problem. Concentrate on a solution that moves you forward.

3

LEADING THE EAGLE WAY

A mother eagle nurtures her young until she sees they are ready to fly. Then she soars high, swoops out from under the eaglet, and allows them to fall again and again until they find their wings. A strong leader knows when it's time to allow others to spread their wings to soar into their next level of growth and success.

Problems are opportunities disguised as challenges to help you learn and grow."

CHAPTER 10

MAKING WAVES

Victory was making waves that took my competitors by surprise. Their perception was that I would appeal to the potential customers using my woman-owned status and expected me to sit back and wait for them to call. They didn't know, or even the customers initially, that I had a different plan entirely. My customers learned quickly that my goals and business plan were to help solve their problems, to be competitive with the best delivery of quality products, and all to be accomplished under the umbrella of a certified woman-owned company. Not only did I convince those in purchasing what a difference we could make, I also worked my way through everyone involved in the supply chain, building a relationship of trust and value. Yes, Victory was making waves and I was determined to turn them into a tsunami.

We were making a name for ourselves. From customers like Duke Energy and Soft Play, it was positive. Words like "service-oriented," "conscientious," and "quality-minded" were commonplace throughout the utility industry.

Sticks and Stones

However, competitors on the scene much larger than us were using other descriptions. Some names were only slightly offensive, and some were quite humorous. Being called a pushy, feminist b-tch seemed to be a compliment—at least in my mind. They knew the customers were seeing me as passionate, confident, and diligently responding to their needs, which ultimately meant making competitors look bad.

Competitors were clearly nervous about my continued success, and one competitor in particular was especially focused on harming our reputation with rumors and assumptions. The rumors are what stung the most because they brought my integrity in to question, including suggesting that I was not indeed a certified woman-owned company. Competitors were implying to customers that this was my husband's company, or encouraging customers to ask who is really "calling the shots" for the company? The most prevailing was that Victory was actually my father's company.

I could have obsessed over the negative, or I could do as my parents did. I would prove I was a tenacious entrepreneur, a leader who followed through by actions and deeds, and not hollow words.

The Sweetest Revenge

The best revenge was a man named Steve, who knocked on my door one Monday morning unannounced. My biggest competitive adversary and loudest critic had employed him. He had left the competitor to build a US market for a German-owned manufacturer. It was a unique product in the United States, and the potential market share was massive. Though they would have a meager beginning, he would build a facility to manufacture their equipment within eighteen months. This equipment was used in the construction and renovation of nuclear and non-nuclear power plants worldwide and would open many doors to new customers for us as well.

This gentleman had also worked previously with Duke. He came to see me for two reasons. Duke was praising the job we were doing, using words like "very service-oriented" and "conscientious," and his previous boss was using adjectives that were not so positive. He told me that "Victory Bolt & Specialty" and "Renee" were dominating their meeting discussions. His boss's thoughts were consumed with ways to beat us because he had quickly learned that pricing alone would not do it and that his derogatory comments were getting him nowhere.

This new customer approached Victory because he preferred a supplier with a steadfast service reputation over his former employer, which bashed their competitors rather than choosing to compete on their own merit. Yes, getting this significant customer was the best revenge.

Our growing pains were real. Though this customer came to us quickly, it also brought a lot of problems disguised as opportunities to learn and grow. We spent a few weeks lining up the business model specifically for them, identifying what their new factory would need from us, and we began putting the quality processes in place and aligning vendors to supply their component parts.

Their orders were coming in faster than expected and larger than anticipated. At first, it was exciting until I was maxing out my line of credit. Without the cash or the line of credit, I would have to tell him I couldn't supply his latest purchase order. Because it was a new commodity and these were new vendors to us, I had to pay large deposits for our first orders, and it would be sixty days before the material arrived and thirty more for the customer to pay. I had pleaded unsuccessfully with the suppliers for extended credit, who ultimately agreed that I would be on a completely open account after this order, which wouldn't help me right then. The bank said no because they had just increased my line to $50,000.00, so I had no choice but to call the customer.

Worst-Case Scenario

My stomach was in knots as I headed into my office and closed my door, which was rare. I called Steve and I explained how much their business meant to us and how much we were growing because they trusted us to give us this opportunity. Then I said, however, that it was causing growing pains I could not overcome for a few months.

In that instant, like a flash through my brain, I remembered how honesty and teamwork had presented long-term relationships when I first breathed life into Victory. I proposed the worst-case scenario by suggesting I needed to turn down the order due to cash flow problems.

His response? "What do you need to make this happen?" I didn't say a word for a minute, which was rare for me as he awaited my pause, thinking it through while on the phone with him. I squeezed my eyes closed as tight as I could and did some quick math. With the profit I had built in, with a 50 percent deposit on his purchase order, I could pay the vendor his share and have some left over for other expenses. So, I did it. I asked for a 50 percent deposit. I didn't stop there. My line of credit was at a much higher percentage rate than giving up a few points for an early payment, so I offered 1 percent-10 Days, Net 30. He countered at 2 percent and our new business arrangement was successfully in the books.

That experience resulted in a strict policy to never say anything negative about a competitor. On many occasions, it had not gone unnoticed, and we were many times complimented on this aspect of how we conducted ourselves respectfully. This was just one instance of how I and my entire team grew exponentially. From product knowledge to servicing one of the most demanding customers we had to date, we grew not just in size, but as a team.

By this time, we desperately needed space again. In passing, I mentioned it to a customer two doors down. He looked at me and said that he would love to downsize. We discussed the square footage and did a walk-through of both locations. We went into my office and called our landlord and discussed our thoughts. Within twenty-four hours, we signed the paperwork for a simple swap of the leases in place. We minimized downtime to relocate the majority of the material and equipment over a long weekend. Little did I know that with this simple move, my dreams of a truly successful company were about to come true.

I had been selling products to several of the same customers I had since I was working for others in the industry. We were growing and many of them were as well. We had truly found our niche for higher-end customers using special materials and products. The marine industry was especially lucrative. The initial customer in Knoxville had now grown to four locations in the Knoxville area, three in Florida, and several others across the country. My dad literally drove their material from Charlotte to their locations every week and put it away on their shelves, while making a handwritten list of what they would need to have delivered the following week. It was tedious, but it was working.

Then, just when you think you are set for a time, your phone rings and your business has the potential to grow beyond your wildest imagination, or you could lose your core customer base and be forced to begin again.

LESSONS TO SOAR

Show what you can do. Actions and deeds matter most. Lead with your actions, demonstrating your value. Doing what you promise you will do carries more weight than any piece of paper, degree, or certification.

Emphasize your positives. Playing up your strengths is far more effective than bashing your competition. It keeps you focused on the positive instead of dwelling on the negative. It also positions you in a more positive, trustworthy light.

The best revenge is earning trust. Don't allow negativity from others to distract you or weaken your resolve. Focus on staying true to building trust and value, and you will prevail.

"You can either curl up in fear or get up and fight."

CHAPTER 11

GROWING PAINS

The call I received was from Russ, the VP of Purchasing, with an opportunity that could take my company and the entire marine industry by storm. They and their largest competitor were being purchased to form one of the largest boat conglomerates in the US at that time. There were approximately twenty factories stretched all across the country, and there I sat with one location in Charlotte, North Carolina.

It was a gut-wrenching moment when I could hardly breathe, excited on one hand and looking around thinking I was going to be sick on the other. These are the times where you curl up in fear, or you get up and fight. I'm not ashamed to say that I curled up in fear for a few days and got myself caught up once again in "what if land," thinking of every possible negative outcome there could be. Then it hit me. I could accept this as a setback or use it as a setup for better things to come. That slight mind shift was enough to get my brain focused on how it could look, and how my company could grow if I got up and fought to win it.

Our biggest assets were our internal team and the service we provided. As long as we were providing quality products, we didn't have to be the lowest price. The types of clients we were most successful with looked at the total package provided, not just the line item cost of the product. The best part was we were partnering with companies that had the same views and values.

I was blessed to have several customers that also were mentors to me, though they really didn't know it. One in particular stands out the most. He helped me by speaking frankly about what we needed to do to be a successful supplier to them. Russ had risen to his rank over the years and was a man of great integrity that treated everyone as an equal and with respect.

As a woman in a man's world, this was most refreshing and made me work even harder to reach every goal. He always offered the facts and honest feedback on how we could both be successful at what we were trying to achieve as a team. He taught me that if I asked the right questions, we could devise a win-win opportunity for all parties every time.

With this in mind, I knew that, first things first, I had to get a seat at the table. So I was now heading off to Knoxville for a face-to-face meeting. I couldn't have hoped for that meeting to have gone better. By asking a list of questions, not only did I get that invitation to "the party," I received insight into what the final decision-making team would expect from the contract winner. The top three bidders would be invited to the corporate location in Chicago to present.

They were looking to go with one supplier and my mind went crazy with ideas. I couldn't sleep or eat. I had to figure this out. With the right negotiations and volume, I can achieve that piece. But the service and logistics pieces would be the bigger nuts to crack.

Grocery Clerk Inspiration

My mind was consumed with how to make this work. While in the grocery store, I looked over from where I was standing and asked a young man scanning merchandise, "What are you doing?" Right there, in one of my least favorite places—the grocery store—that sixteen-year-old boy gave me the solution I was searching for.

He said, "I'm scanning this label and then typing in the number of cans of green beans we need that are somehow reaching the people that will send them to us."

I'll never forget how he looked at me for asking him that question, but more than that, how excited I got as he explained it. I know he must have thought I was crazy.

My customer had spoken very frankly to me when we met that day. He told me, "You need to figure out a way to be in our facilities without increasing labor costs and at the same time controlling or even decreasing freight costs." I remember looking at him like he had two heads, but I knew I would have to figure it out. And I just did.

The request for quotation (RFQ) came in certified mail as promised. It was a complete package with all of their plant locations that we were to serve, and the actual list of items with annual volumes was displayed on a very expansive

Lotus 1-2-3 spreadsheet. Greg, one of the best inside salespeople that I ever had, looked at me and we began laughing. We knew our work was cut out for us on every level. We didn't even have Lotus, much less know how to use it. Lotus, the spreadsheet software before Office 365 was ever invented, was what larger companies used. We didn't have it yet. We were still old school. So that meant while we were getting costs and putting the pricing together manually, I was going to publishing companies to get ideas and quotes on my presentation.

We were definitely the underdogs, but we would not let anyone else know it. We would fight until the end, and we were going to enjoy every minute.

While I was researching what I had seen in the grocery store, my team began putting together the bid packages by commodity for our vendors. It wasn't long until word got out about the opportunity and who was bidding for the package. Vendors began ringing our phones and coming to see us to get a shot at the opportunity as well. Our sourcing options were growing, but I also knew that each one of these potential vendors had their favorite incumbents. More sources didn't necessarily make us more competitive, but it would give us insight into raw material availability as well as an overall look at the market structure.

After numerous phone calls, I found a software company in Atlanta that could create what I needed to do with the service tracking portion of the contract. It was not currently used in the industrial market, but it was well known in the grocery and drug industries. He could write a program specifically for us and then work with our current software and hardware companies to get it implemented. The process, however, would take six months to complete.

With no internet to rely on, you could take more liberties in your presentations. I say this because even though it may not have been completely ethical, I took photos from a vendor's massive warehouse that was packed from floor to ceiling with inventory and shiny new racks. There would be no evidence left behind after I departed because I put my presentation on slides and displayed it on a screen. I pondered again and again about whether I should use these photos, but in the end, I used them. I would have this type of facility one day and I just needed to stay in the game until I could make it happen. This sizeable contract would do just that.

As we prepared to submit the pricing, we wrapped the entire project in prayer. If this was going to be successful, it needed much more strength and knowledge than we had alone. We were the least in size of all those looking this opportunity in the face, but that didn't mean we were not the best choice.

Victory Bolt & Specialty may not have had robust tools or equal the size of our giant competitors, but we had tenacity, enterprising creativity, and a relentlessly driven purpose with our eye on the prize. I was determined not to see the curves or the bumps ahead but to see the checkered flag at the end of the race. Spoken like a diehard NASCAR fan! In my mind, we had the advantage. The other contenders considered us the underdogs, and this blatant underestimation of our capabilities only fueled the fire in my gut. I would use the adversity I had faced in the past, put one foot in front of the other, and wrap this opportunity in prayer with our entire team. Others in the industry never saw us coming up behind them, but they would eventually see us pull ahead. I challenged everyone to keep their eyes on the prize and have a little faith.

Going For It All

The call came in and we were competitive enough to get us to Chicago to present. All the potential suppliers were scheduled to visit on the same day at different times. On presentation day, I sat in the lobby alone in my brand new red skirt and jacket as the owner of my major competitor and his team descended the stairs.

I was so nervous. My palms were sweating and I was shaking. I saw him coming over and I removed my hand from my briefcase where I had stuck some tissue to wipe my hand. He said, "I see you came alone."

I replied, "I can get the job done just fine."

"Since the contract is so large, I think they will split the contract. What do you think?"

"I haven't thought about that as an option. Victory is going for the entire contract."

His eyes got wide as he looked over his shoulder and said goodbye. My nerves calmed as I smiled and waved, because I had work to do, and I headed up the beautiful, winding stainless steel staircase.

I walked into the conference room and set up my slide projector for my presentation. The table was long, made of dark mahogany, and had sixteen high-back chairs around it. Each chair was filled with men from around the country that represented each manufacturing facility. Some were in purchasing, some from their quality departments, and others were from logistics. There was only one female in the room that represented purchasing. I took a moment and breathed it all in. It had taken a while, but I was back in Corporate America doing what I loved. And no longer was I in the dingy, dark warehouses where it all began.

As they pummeled me with question after question, I showed them the facts about what we could offer that seemed to satisfy each department. Now, I was tasked with returning home and waiting as they finalized their bid calculations and to determine who would do their site visit and when.

As we waited, worked on other opportunities, and carried on business as usual, a natural disaster occurred halfway around the world. An earthquake in Kobe, Japan, could derail everything. I was watching nickel pricing begin to rise on the raw materials market. Nickel is used in the production of stainless steel. This entire process would be for nothing if a decision was not made sooner rather than later to capture the necessary inventory.

I pushed the customer to make a decision when the call came in that they wanted to make a site visit to Victory Bolt & Specialty, Inc. a week from that day.

LESSONS TO SOAR

"What if land" gets you nowhere fast. Don't waste time and brainpower on all that could go wrong. Envision and put your energy around all that could go right. When what appears to be a setback occurs, use it as a setup for better things to come.

Embrace the 3 Cs. Success requires the ability to ***connect*** with others and ***collaborate*** to ***create*** an extraordinary outcome that otherwise may not be possible. Teamwork makes the dream work.

Shared values raise your worth. The right people, teams, and partners reveal themselves through their actions and how they live through their word. When values align, what seems impossible becomes divinely empowered.

“Your willpower has the power to move decisions in your favor.”

CHAPTER 12

VICTORY IS SWEET

We were operating on a "wing and a prayer" literally. We may have been preparing to wow the marine industry, but we were flying high in having earned the next step toward winning this contract and also flying by the seat of our pants to make it all come together and work in time for their visit. What is the saying . . . "be careful what you wish for"?

We cleaned and organized. We went through our quality processes with a fine-tooth comb. Every employee was drilled with questions they may be asked, and we gave one last review to our offer to make sure we had missed nothing. Still, something was missing. We had racked this entire warehouse, and there was a great deal of vacant space on the shelves. We had ample inventory for our current customers and were showing ample room to grow, but I felt we needed to show a larger availability of inventory on our shelves.

Then it hit me! Have you read the book about Sam Walton, the founder of Walmart? I did many years ago, and a method that he used to make a good impression long before he was a huge success stood out to me as something we also had to do. He used empty appliance boxes that suited his needs for a retail store to appear as if he had far more inventory than he actually had. I thought if it worked for him, it might for us. The day before the scheduled site visit, we had several employees taping up empty boxes. In eight hours, they made over 300 boxes that we sat on the pallets behind our actual inventory. We couldn't have an empty box being knocked off the shelf tipping our hand.

Stacked in Our Favor

There was only one thing left on my mind. Did we have enough employees to show we could handle the dramatic increase in sales? Well, my creative mind—or some might have classified as my crazy mind—went into overdrive and I got employees from the neighboring businesses to "work" at Victory for the day.

You may be judging me right now, but I looked at it like I had one shot, so I would give it all we had. I knew we would be a great supplier for them and once we were awarded the contract, the boxes would be filled, and employees would be hired to become a part of the Victory team.

The big day came. The corporate team joined us from various locations across the country and they stayed most of the day. It was a very, very long day. They had individuals that spent time in all departments reviewing the automated replenishment program we were developing. I knew that would be high on their list during the informal audit, so I had asked the software manufacturer to fly in as well to help support us. The day went well, and it was my policy early on to always, always, ask for the order.

As the final site visitor was walking out the door, I asked the big question, "Are we getting the contract?"

With a big smile that I will never forget, he said, "It's yours. But you can't tell anyone until I let the others know they were not awarded the contract."

I really tried to keep it quiet, but mother and daddy saw me later that night and they said, "You got it, didn't you?"

"Why do you ask?"

"It's written all over your face," my mom said.

The peace in my heart and the smile from excitement on my face could not be hidden. We had been blessed beyond my imagination and I was so very thankful.

One week later, everyone from Victory came to our home for a party—and celebrate we did. We enjoyed champagne and a large vanilla and chocolate cake that was decorated with a large yacht with VB&S written on it and a smaller sinking ship with the main competitor's name on it we had defeated.

Obstacle after Obstacle

Now, it was time for the really arduous work to begin. There was so much to do—starting with notifying our chosen suppliers of our award and intentions. The metal market price increase was turning into a dire situation. We had bought the greatest portion of our material from the largest stainless steel fastener importer in the United States. They had buying power like no other and they could get the factories in Taiwan to take their orders while others could not. Together, we could pull this off.

The earthquake in Japan would create a shortage of material in the supply chain that had not occurred in years. That wasn't all. Competitors were still trying to take us down. I got a phone call from Bruce, the president of the importing company, and he indicated he had received a phone call from my competitor that had lost the contract bid. The competitor asked him not to honor their pricing to us and that if they did not, the bid would have to go back out for current pricing. It was gratifying when Bruce said that he just laughed at him and said, "You just need to understand you just lost. She outsold you." This further solidified the lesson to never talk negatively about the competition. It also confirmed to never underestimate them either.

The next hurdle was to go back to the bank to take care of the new line of credit I would need for these types of volume purchases. With my new formal contract in hand, the meeting was set for their corporate offices in Charlotte. This size of request was pushed up the ladder from the local level and I was introduced to a whole new team of bankers. They had already done their due diligence, and we were approved to move up from the $50,000 credit line to the $1 million credit line. Though there would be a new banker in my future, John was there as well. When asked why he took a chance on me, he said, "When

I first met Renee, she didn't have a pot to pee in. But she knew the industry and had a willpower strong enough to do it. And she did."

The room erupted into laughter and as I was laughing with them, I said under my breath, "Thank you, God!" And for the first time in a meeting, I'm sure they saw the tears in my eyes, but those were tears of pure joy!

We had scheduled a launch date on the contract based on their current vendor's material availability, which equated to the usual import time frame of four months. With the earthquake, supply was in very short supply in the US and containers from the ports were running more like five to six months, if we were lucky. To make matters worse, factories could take orders at higher prices, and that put us in danger as well. Once again, the contract was in jeopardy, and I was going to be forced into asking for a price increase before we had established supplying the first customer site.

Looking back, we were like Moses in the desert. The Red Sea was the customer, and the Egyptians were the competitors coming behind us and we had nowhere to turn. There we were with what seemed like no way forward and it was of no fault of our making.

I'd never had an issue as big as this one, but I knew what I had to do. I made the call to the VP of Purchasing, and it was not received well. At least it was on a Friday, but I'm not sure if that made it any better. It was a long weekend awaiting the next conversation on Monday afternoon.

Praying for a Miracle

I can remember that weekend quite vividly. We lived in the country about thirty minutes from the nearest town. I did little relaxing. I couldn't sit still. I was a nervous wreck. Had it all been for nothing? Would I fail? I was mortified. I spent my time cutting grass, riding go-carts with Heather, pressure washing the deck and sidewalks, and I bet I walked thirty miles around that one-acre pond. Thankfully, I also spent a great deal of time reading my Bible, every devotion about fear I could get my hands on, and prayed. Yes, I prayed and prayed and prayed. I said, "God, you brought me this far and I know you will not leave me now. Please make a way where I see none."

I got to work on Monday and gathered the team. We had been working diligently for weeks trying to solve the supply issue while we were waiting on our import material to arrive, but to no avail. Any material that was readily available was at costs even higher than we had quoted. Then, about 10:00 a.m., God showed up in a big way.

A former supplier for my contract customer was getting out of the marine industry and was willing to sell us a truckload of the specific material we were needing. My purchasing manager said he sat there, holding his breath waiting for the catch. There was no catch. They even sold us the material at the costs they had paid, which was 25 percent below the current market value. It would be delivered to our door within ten days.

But God wasn't done yet. Before I could make the call that afternoon, the VP of Purchasing called me and said, "Thank you for the call on Friday and letting me know what we are up against." He did his research over the weekend and the price increase we were asking for is miniscule compared to what is happening in the industry.

I said, "Thank you so much, but this morning, we received a blessing and could solve a sizeable portion of the supply chain issue. Because of this purchase, the price increase will be even less than we discussed on Friday and with only a few items."

I know he was surprised. And yes, I could have kept our "recently found" inventory at very competitive costs a secret and gotten a price increase at the same time. For me, honesty has always served me well when negotiating, and especially at the onset of a relationship where trust is being truly built.

This was a long-term relationship and fairness was the name of the game for me, and with his response to my call, I knew he agreed. He told me to fax him the details as soon as possible and he would update the contract pricing effective immediately. I'm not sure if I was more thankful that day or the day the contract was awarded. It was all a part of the journey that God had set me on.

LESSONS TO SOAR

Demonstrate what you can become. Be willing to stretch yourself to demonstrate what you are capable of accomplishing. When others see, they quickly believe.

When you put others first, they'll put you first. It is always long after your focus on doing what is in the best interests of others that you receive your reward. It begins with doing it because it was the right thing to do.

Patience is a virtue. God's timing is not the same as ours. Our perceived timelines, clouded judgments, and opinions of others do not hamper Him. The wait may seem impossible, but worth it.

Faith makes the fight worthwhile. In order to draw strength from adversity, use your faith as a tool to see you through. You too will learn that victory is sweet when you use your fighting spirit to deny defeat.

"He will cover you with his feathers. He will shelter you with his wings. His faithful promises are your armor and protection."

—Psalm 91:4

"When you think you are ready, you are not."

CHAPTER 13

BACKUP PLAN

During the due diligence phase for the contract several months earlier, I was asked a question that left me speechless, which doesn't happen often. The question was, "What happens if you die?"

Is anyone really ever prepared for that question, especially in a business meeting? My first thought was, 'I'm going to heaven.' But I had a feeling that was not what he meant. He was referring to a succession plan, a backup plan, that I did not have. I'm so thankful that he asked me that question. It helped me realize the need, and I put a plan into place for the future and the longevity of the company. Little did I know how much I would need it.

Once again, God's timing was perfect because soon thereafter, I would face a situation that changed things dramatically. It was another divine intervention timed exactly when I needed it, even though I didn't realize it fully at the time.

I had signed up to walk through the largest boat show in the United States, which included making a presentation for a potentially large marine customer specializing in fishing boats. Many of my current customers and potential customers would be there as well. My business had become a true family affair. My mom had come to work for Victory to fill an accounting position. I decided it would be a great mother-daughter getaway as well. So off we went to Chicago.

Competitors and Their Games

The presentation went well, or so I thought. Then the customer asked if he could call me later that day. I then got another shock at how low companies and their employees would stoop. He informed me I had to get them bank details because another competitor that I had beaten previously on a large contract told them I had overextended myself and was headed toward insolvency. Now, rather than just considering what we had to offer, including the stellar letters of recommendation from two other boat builders and from the bank that we were in good financial standing, I was in the position where I had to defend my company from this absolute slander.

But should I?

Another customer, Richard, had just called me the week prior with the fantastic news that they were turning their entire contract over to Victory. I had been on a trial basis with fill-in orders for several months. I asked him, "What did we do that led to your decision?"

"Your company has been doing things the right way and your competitor failed by behaving inappropriately."

Richard had been using the same supplier for several years and said it had shocked him and felt he needed to speak frankly, so I was prepared for what was being said in the industry.

I could tell from the beginning of working with Richard that he was a man of integrity with his suppliers and was very fair at doing business. The owner of my biggest competitor had made remarks about my looks and that my customer was probably giving me some orders because I had legs up to my neck. For Richard, this behavior undermined the other vendor's credibility and his respect for them. Because he stood up and demanded upstanding vendors, he and his boss agreed to pull their contract and made us their preferred supplier. Yet another example of how ***not*** bashing the competition leads to the win.

Time and time again, I was being reminded that business and the world in general can be ruthless. I came to understand that the relationships that would be the most successful and long-term would be with those that conduct themselves using a similar moral compass.

In Our Best Interests

From meetings with my team and through much prayer, I decided it was in the company's best interest to remove us from the contract consideration for the company requesting my financials. I and my banker did not need to put ourselves in a position for our character to be scrutinized because of innuendo and rumors spread by their current supplier. I was sure God would provide customers that were better suited for our long-term mission, like the one that we had just landed. Already having the newly awarded contract, I never regretted my decision, and it wouldn't be the last time I walked away from the negotiating table refusing to do business with a company that was not in our best interest.

My mom and I had a great trip to Chicago. It was wonderful to get away with time to walk along Lake Michigan and visit the Sears Tower. We rode the fastest elevator in the world to the observation deck and took in breathtaking views unlike any we had ever seen before. The business portion of the trip had not gone as well as hoped, but I had made some great contacts, shook hands, and expressed my gratitude to many current customers. Even getting lost in a not-so-great neighborhood on the outskirts of Chicago at 4:30 a.m. after checking out of our hotel turned out to be an adventure and provided a few laughs as well.

We missed our plane, but we laughed because it provided an excellent opportunity for some fantastic shopping. We took a later flight and got bumped to first class, where we drank champagne and discussed how independent we felt in this big city and how different life had become since leaving Marshville several years before. I said to my mother, "If I die today, I'm ready. My life has been wonderful, and I am blessed."

I thought I meant it. And I did at the time, but three days later, I would let my impatience get the best of me. I would later regret what I said, asking God for more time, that I was wrong. I still had more to do if He would let me.

LESSONS TO SOAR

Your guiding principles won't steer you wrong. Business and the world in general can be ruthless. You don't have to be. You can win with your character, valor, and values intact.

See a setback as a setup for success. Learning to see adversity as a setup for something great rather than a setback for disaster is a powerful mind shift. It will strengthen your resolve and lift you to higher ground to soar. Always ask yourself, Is this happening to me or for me?

Be replaceable, and you are unstoppable. Nurturing others to step into your shoes is the fastest way for you to take flight to even greater heights. Being irreplaceable is holding yourself back.

"When it comes to your money, always be in the know."

CHAPTER 14

A TAXING SITUATION

On a Monday morning, several months before heading to Chicago, my assistant came into my office looking like she had seen a ghost, alerting me that there were two men in the lobby asking for me. I asked who they were, and she said, "One has a shiny gold badge and here's his card." He was from the South Carolina Department of Revenue. What could I say, except but "send them in"?

The young man was dressed in an all-black suit, shirt, and tie and he was with another gentleman who was dressed more casual with very little to say, and barely making eye contact.

They informed me I was negligent in paying South Carolina sales tax for the last three years. I explained that couldn't be because what I bought was tax exempt because of my resale certificate that I had my assistant present. He said they had concerns we were not charging South Carolina residents when they bought goods directly from our counter for walk-in customers, as they would be considered retail and not exempt as a direct sale. I was at a loss for words. After three hours of being made to feel like a criminal, with it being made clear tax evasion was punishable by law with fines and possible jail time, I called my attorney. After instructions from him, I asked them to leave if there was nothing further. I wanted my attorney present, and I needed time to consult my accounting firm that had been managing my financials and taxes. It felt like something out of a crime show, with me being in the spotlight. Once again, I was sick to my stomach.

Mistakes Happen

I made phone calls back to the attorney and our accountant while enlisting the help of my internal accounting team, led by my mother. She was confused as to what she had been seeing from the accountants showing we didn't owe any South Carolina taxes and was horrified for her only child. I was pretty nervous and trying not to stress out from anticipatory anxiety or go to "what if land" again. I had run the company above board, hiring the necessary people to take care of these types of things on my behalf. What had gone wrong? I had meetings set up for the following day.

In short order, we learned that the accounting firm had been writing off tiny amounts of sales tax from our city counter. These sales were less than 5 percent of our total sales and South Carolina customers made up an even smaller amount of dollars. But, over three years, it looked like I was evading taxes. My attorney thought that this information would suffice for them to recalculate and to pay the taxes accordingly. But I also learned from the auditor dressed in the casual attire that first visit, that this was the young man-in-black's first case in the field and he was out to make a name for himself. "Great!" I said under my breath.

The audit was scheduled to begin Wednesday, the week after my mother and I returned from the trade show in Chicago. I had delegated the task of pulling all the files to be done while I was away and returned to find the task had not been done. I was angry and, rather than delegating the task again, I thought I would just do it myself. I took matters into my hands, not realizing I would pay an enormous price.

I got my daddy to help me and ascended the ladder to an area fifteen feet high in the warehouse where the records were stored. The building was old, and the flooring was not stable. The next thing I heard as I reached for a box was the cracking of the boards under the ladder. As I struggled to find a place to grab, the rotted floorboards gave way. I cried, "Daddy!" as I plummeted on to the concrete floor below, landing flat on my back.

Not Ready to Die

The pain was excruciating, and the ambulance was called as my employees, mom, and daddy looked down on me. Tears were rolling down my face, which made my pain even worse. All I could do was pray.

"Dear Lord, I'm sorry I said I was ready to die. I'm not ready. Please give me some more time."

Then, staying true to form, I saw my best salesperson standing there with wide eyes and a pale face. In that instant, I reviewed my "to do lists" in my head and appointments for the rest of the week and shouted out directives to my team. I had to make sure they handled everything as promised. They all laughed and said, "She's going to be OK!"

All I knew was it hurt so badly, and thinking about other things seemed to make it less painful. The ambulance arrived and they began asking questions, flashing a light in my eyes, and other normal things a medic would do. They were sticking me with needles all over my body, asking, "Can you feel this? Can you feel that?" I said, "Yes," and I thought to myself, "Thank you, God!" I could feel everything. They put on a neck brace and slid me on the backboard and off we went.

The MRI revealed I broke my back in three places. I would spend the next three months in a hospital bed in my living room to minimize the pain for the and ease of putting my brace on and off. When I went to the doctor after three weeks of wearing a back brace, he said that I didn't have to worry about paralysis any longer. I asked, "What do you mean?"

"Until the bones set in place, you were in danger of the bones touching nerves that could result in you losing feeling in your legs and your ability to walk. If you had known, you may have been afraid to move and then your bones would have set incorrectly, and you would have faced surgery."

I was shocked. I had not understood all of this, but was so thankful at the same time.

In true form, however, I was also calling on customers and working with the employees in the office day in and day out via the phone. I told myself it kept my mind occupied, but I still wasn't ready to admit I was a workaholic and give up my addiction cold turkey, if at all.

Because I had been stuck in bed for so many months, I had to rebuild every muscle in my back that had atrophied because of no activity from the brace holding me together. The physical therapy was grueling, but I knew the harder I worked, the sooner my life would return to normal.

I went back to work first part-time and then full time long before I should have. I went to physical therapy every day in the nearby hospital rehab center, and before I knew it, I was getting stronger. It wasn't long before I was working the same as before.

Like I Was Never Gone

I never forgot what that big contract customer asked me during their due diligence because I thought about it often while slowly recovering. After returning to work full time, I called him and asked, "Do you remember asking me what happens if I die?"

"Yes," he said.

"Well, I didn't die, but I broke my back."

"What's going to happen to our service and your company?"

I proudly shared: "Nothing will change. In fact, everything is fine. It happened three months ago, and you didn't even know I wasn't there."

I then thanked him for his question, and admitted I thought it was crazy at the time. However, it was exactly what I needed to hear to inspire the succession plan that had been put in place—proving beneficial for times just like this. Many times in my career, I used this experience to make him feel good about helping my company be more efficient along the way and how he had contributed to the success. It was a proud and thankful day for me, and I made sure all of my team knew all they had done to make it happen.

This could have and should have been a tipping point in my life. However, I still had not learned my lesson. God had a lot more lessons in store for me, and they certainly would come to light later on. If He couldn't get my full attention with this potentially life-altering event, there would be others that would attempt to stop me in my tracks.

For now, I had to get back to work. I had a business to run, and customers and employees were depending on me. Besides, I still had a little thing called tax evasion hanging over my head. While I was recuperating, the auditor was fast at work going through all the invoices and recording any details where my accountants had not instructed us to pay the South Carolina sales tax.

Three Years Add Up

It may have seemed like miniscule dollars to the accounting firm when looking at it month by month, but it quickly added up during the audit. In working with my attorney, I learned that the bottom line was whether the state of South Carolina could prove that I had ***deliberately*** tried to cheat them out of this money or it was truly unknown to me.

Once the state completed their audit, they had a dollar amount I owed, and still had not relinquished their idea that I had willingly defrauded them. After penalties and fines, the total went from the approximate $8000.00 owed that had been just "written off" to over $34,000.00 with penalties! They were investigating a three-year time period and if you think about that, it was approximately $250.00 per month. Small dollars in the eyes of the accountants, but certainly not in the eyes of the people that were owed the money, and rightfully so, as I admitted repeatedly during all their interrogations. I would explain, "If I had known, why wouldn't I have paid you like I had paid North Carolina and my federal taxes as required? And they are all current."

There was one last meeting to determine the final outcome and whether they were going to prosecute. It was a very scary day, to say the least, but this time I lost my patience. We assembled in a large conference room in my attorney's office in uptown Charlotte. There were eight people present, including me, the lead investigator, the auditor, my attorney, and the two owners of the accounting firm, and my mom. Isn't it funny how, though I told myself my mom was there as my accounting supervisor, even at the age of thirty-four, I needed her desperately to be by my side? Plainly put, I needed my mother.

The accountant admitted to their error in judgment and full guilt in the matter. However, the lead investigator was still wearing his hat of intimidation and his ego on his sleeve with threats of a trial and potential jail time. I had enough of this and said, "If you have enough incriminating evidence—which you don't—to take this to trial, then do it. I'm done."

As I looked at my mom, we both stood up to leave, when I noticed two things—my attorney's look of fear, but then a grin on the auditor's face. He knew something that the rest of us didn't. A few seconds later, the investigator asked me to sit back down and continue negotiations. That day we settled on a lesser amount of $25,000.00 to be paid immediately and the case would be closed.

What a relief! And this time, my impatience didn't get me into trouble. It was an opportunity to stand up for myself because I knew I was not guilty of what I was being accused of doing. I know, without a shadow of doubt, that God gave me the courage to do what I did that day, and He knew all along how it would turn out.

This was a huge lesson to me, to always have a great outside supportive team that you trust, but always—yes, always—verify the information they are providing you. From then on, when we submitted our monthly computer-generated financial statements for them to reconcile, it was checked with a "fine-tooth comb." The accountants, after seeing what we had gone through and admitting they were negligent, agreed to pay all the penalties and late fees. This level of accountability on their part resulted in them remaining our accountants for many years after this event, proving that having partners with similar values will make you all winners in the end. Even when mistakes are made, integrity makes you a true winner.

LESSONS TO SOAR

Mistakes happen. Being accountable isn't always about everything going right and as promised. It is also about making things right when things don't go as expected or understood.

Being a workaholic is an addiction. When you love what you do for a living, it is easy to make excuses. Make sure the excuses being made are not at the expense of those you love or your own well-being and life enjoyment.

"You have seen what I did to the Egyptians. You know how I carried you on eagles' wings and brought you to myself."

—Exodus 19:4

"Never be afraid to ask. The answer might just surprise you."

CHAPTER 15

PLACE TO CALL HOME

Victory was busting out at the seams . . . again.

We had made all the capital improvements we could make to store the amount of inventory that we needed to maintain adequate service and on-time deliveries to our current customer base. The large contract we had obtained was in full swing, with all the locations on board across the country as well as in Mexico and Canada. We had successfully implemented our inventory bar-code program using wireless handheld equipment along with inventory specialists placed strategically across the country. Our customers were using Victory as an example of "best practices" to their other suppliers.

The best part was we were combining shipments to control freight costs and all the material was shipping on a regular replenishment schedule from Charlotte. That meant we could keep our overhead and expenses low because we didn't have extra costs from various locations across the country. We had raised industry standards.

It had not gone flawlessly, but once completed, it was a great distraction from the nightmare that had been my life for over a year. The opportunity to prove that my small company could pull this off successfully had been my driving force during the health adversity as well as during the potential threat of jail from the accused tax evasion. Now, with both of these challenges in my rearview mirror, it was time to focus again on Victory's future as well as mine.

Every day when I would leave work, I would ride around the neighboring county where I lived looking for land or a building for sale. I had a dream that this time, when I relocated, it would be to a facility that I would own and that had the potential to grow and expand if necessary. My goal was that I never wanted to have to move again.

Ask and You Might Receive

It wasn't as easy as I had hoped. Each building that I found was too far into the county to service my current customer base adequately, and buying land to build was just too expensive. Then one day, after several months of looking, I drove by a large open field that advertised thirty-two acres for sale. It was a perfect location, and I immediately called the real estate company. Why I instantly picked up my cell phone and called that day had to be a "God thing" because I only needed two acres. Yes, that's right, two acres. And I was calling about a thirty-two-acre tract for sale.

The realtor confirmed that it was exactly as the sign had indicated, the entire tract of land was for sale, no partials.

The landowner was asking for $6000.00 per acre, which was a great price. My heart stopped because it was even more perfect, but then the realtor said again that the owner would not split the acreage. However, something inside me gave me the courage to ask for what I needed. I knew I would lose this opportunity to own my own location for Victory if I didn't at least ask. The average price per acre I had seen was more than four times this amount and I said, "Will you just ask him to sell me *four* acres?"

With the price he was asking, as compared to the other acreage I had found or building costs I could afford, I decided to ask for four, not two acres. At this cost, I could get more acreage and add on to the facility later as we grew. He said he would ask and call me back. I figured it would be several days before I heard back, but within a few hours, I had my answer.

Yes, he would sell me the four acres, but at a higher price. I held my breath as he said the owner wants $8000.00 per acre. This had been some of the easiest negotiations I had ever experienced, and I knew the timing was right and was an answer to my prayer. I asked him before we hung up to prepare the paperwork as soon as possible. After all, I didn't want him to change his mind!

I made the right decision because when he sold the balance of the plot of land, he realized he had undercharged me, and sold it for the going market value, which was four times what I paid per acre.

Too Many Hats

To save money, I acted as general contractor alongside the design/build firm I had chosen, with me overseeing all aspects of the construction phase. It paid off financially, resulting in a half million dollars in savings. But how much could I have made if I had just done what I was best at doing, which was running Victory, instead of acting as a general contractor? You might be thinking $500,000 is a lot of savings. Yes, it is. But working seventy plus hours a week takes a toll that you cannot put a dollar figure on, especially when you consider where that time could have been spent in business development and time with family.

The building was finished in the time frame promised and it was beautiful. My goal was to have this facility provide a warm and inviting atmosphere where employees would feel comfortable and proud to be a part of the company. After all, they would spend more time here than they did at their home. This included offices reflecting who they were as people as well.

For visitors and customers, I wanted them to see that we were not only faithful to our professional values and mission, but we were also faithful to our Christian values. The area that was most noticed and talked about in the community was the wall that you first saw when you entered the building behind the receptionist's desk. It contained a beautiful 3D image of an eagle in flight carrying a bolt and nut with the letters below that cited Isaiah 40:31.

The first area of decor I completed was our "Wall of Fame" outside my office in the hallway. This was where we hung all of our awards and articles written about us, including framed customer letters of recommendation. Its purpose was to show the pride that we felt for the hard work we put into Victory every day.

The finishing touches to our facility was a family affair too. As the building was being completed, my dad shopped everywhere looking for the best deals on floor-to-ceiling pallet racking and shelving that we would need to maximize the twenty-five thousand square feet that had a very high ceiling capacity. With the proper design and layout, we could accommodate years of growth and never have to move again. Also, to make it even more reassuring that this would be our last move, I had purchased enough acreage to make additions to the existing facility if needed.

While this move had taken us longer than the others, it was laying the groundwork for momentum-building growth.

Business was moving along successfully. Our new location also gave us the ability to buy many products directly from the manufacturer. That's when I had a bright idea of how to make even more profit. This is where burning the candle at both ends can pay off.

LESSONS TO SOAR

Feel out all sides in a negotiation. When you are just seeing your side, you could put yourself at a disadvantage. When you see their side, they are more likely to see yours.

Money saved isn't necessarily money earned. Know what time is costing you along with what it could bring you in greater value spent elsewhere. If you are spending all your time to save money, you may actually cost yourself money and relationships.

Make your work environment inviting. Most likely you spend more hours working than you do sleeping. Make the space you work in a place that inspires and appreciates you being there.

4

LEADING THE EAGLE WAY

Eagles take great care in building their nests to nurture their young. While they prefer tall trees, they are adaptable to their surroundings when the terrain is formidable to their desires. Leaders must be agile, able to adapt to situations and circumstances for future growth and increased productivity.

"It is not what we do that determines who we are. It is who we are that determines what we do."

CHAPTER 16

CULTURE CLASH

Our customer base was in a steady growth mode, and I decided it was time to forge ahead with a major concentration on improving margins. I had been gathering details on the quality manufacturers that were providing us with products through our current supply chain. I knew cutting out the middleman and buying direct myself was key. I knew who the players were, and I knew I had the volumes to get their attention, but I needed to learn how to do business in Asia.

I had the necessary legal paperwork completed for my new LLC, an import company called Exclusive Industrial Imports. As I began my research, it shocked me to learn that it was difficult for women to come to the table to negotiate in other parts of the world. But I had an idea. I had taken on a different identity prior to owning my own company in my career, and maybe I should do it again. Thus, "Charlie Hart" was born.

During these days, before the internet, you did research via catalogs and quality assurance documents and testimonials. You asked for samples and placed small purchase orders to test their products and to test how they would meet delivery commitments. This proved effective and the fax machine was humming with my new company, receiving product expansion inquiries that kept growing and growing.

I strategically created a different company and contact name because I didn't want my current suppliers to know that I was buying direct. I would still need them as a backup source and for any new items that might arise. I wanted to make sure that we kept our competitive edge with them as well. After all, I couldn't import everything, and I understood the value of maintaining these relationships.

At some point, you must put a face with a fax and wire transfers. As we grew to forty-foot container loads of material flowing into our loading docks from Taiwan, a trip was planned. Because I knew it was not always successful for women to do business abroad during this time period, I gave Robert a crash course. For several weeks, I tried to teach him who the factories were and what they made. As time grew closer, I knew that him posing as "Charlie" was going to put the relationships I was trying to build in jeopardy, and I had to take a chance on revealing being a woman at the helm. I needed to come clean and show that it really didn't matter that a woman ran the company. What mattered was that we could perform and be a strong import partner.

Charlie Hart Revealed

One of our best vendors met us at the airport. Their VP of Sales was a lady, and her name was Alicia. We laughed and laughed when she went to shake Robert's hand only to discover that I was "Charlie." It was a pleasant surprise for her as much as it was for me. We had a lot to talk about as I gave her a large fluffy teddy bear wearing a T-shirt of the American flag. She later told me it stayed in her Mercedes for years and she had fond memories of that visit. It was rare for her, as well, to have the opportunity to work with another female in our business.

We visited her firm's factory, and she took us sightseeing while also visiting the other factories we were working with at the time. That first night we went to dinner with her and the owner of the factory who hardly spoke English. Early in the evening, a Chinese welcome wine was served in what looked like a shot glass. We all looked at each other, tapped our glasses together, and I downed the "shot."

When I looked up, they had only taken a sip. As we all laughed, she said to me, "Don't feel bad. That's not the first time that has happened." I decided right then and there, I would study customs of other countries more closely in the future.

I learned so much on this trip and it was one of the greatest times of my life. It's hard to explain, but I was in a foreign country with a new name, and I could be anything I wanted to be, even a superhero. I learned that being tall—by their standards—with blonde hair, I resembled one of their superheroes from one of their new video games.

While I'm no superhero by any stretch of the imagination, it brought a less serious side to the trip and made for enduring memories of their stares, smiles, and handshakes when they would pass me on the street. At the end of the day, I may have been called "Charlie," but I decided to just be myself, the person God created me to be, and I knew that would be enough.

I have had long-term relationships with the people of Asia and many still call me "Charlie" to this day. On a side note, my granddaughter is named Charleigh Hart. It brings a smile to my face every time I call her name—using an Asian inflection, of course. I can't wait to tell her this story when she gets older, and we can pretend to be superheroes together.

My youngest, Savannah, was born in July 2000. Her hair was as white as snow and her complexion was very fair, like a porcelain doll. Her eyes were as blue as the sky and as round as saucers. She was beautiful, but more importantly, very healthy, though she was a long, skinny little girl. Because I had a tough pregnancy with Heather, and I was thirty-eight years old, I was told I could expect an even harder time with this one. This did not hold true, and this pregnancy was uneventful and beautiful. Because of where I was in life with the business, I actually took six weeks to be a full-time mom.

Heather was eleven years older than Savannah, so she was there to help every step of the way. She was so excited to have a baby sister. A few moments after she was born, Heather was holding Savannah and looked at me with tears in her eyes and said, "How can you love somebody so much that you just met?" That's a precious moment in my life that will always put a smile on my face and will make my heart swell with love for my girls.

Abuse Has Different Faces

Despite the joy I felt for my work and my daughters, my marriage had unfortunately been crumbling for a while. When Savannah was three, we decided to call it quits. We tried to make it work, including several years of counseling, but to no avail. We were very different people and trying to work together with me at the helm was too hard on him and me.

When someone is jealous of your strengths, they will try to bring you down. They will try to manipulate you into second-guessing your every move. For me, my confidence at work didn't waver, however, in my personal life and the life of my girls, especially Heather as a teenager, it did waver. When you hear constant tirades directed at your character, your self-esteem will diminish, and you begin to believe those lies. It can change you forever if you let it.

I was leading a board meeting at our local battered women's shelter when it occurred to me what was truly going on in my life. I believe God revealed His path to me when I was ready to understand it and when I had a mind clear enough from depression to see it. At that moment, I realized I was in the same pattern from the previous years. History was repeating itself. I had now been in two relationships that were full of jealousy and rage toward who I was as a person. Even though it wasn't physical abuse, it was mental torture. I had realized that even though one is visible, and the other is unseen, both are unacceptable and will seep into the very core of your being and work to destroy you.

The men I was romantically allowing into my life had issues with their own insecurities, and nothing I could do would change that. I tried to change myself to be what would make them feel better about themselves, but I was beginning to realize God made me who I am for His purpose. God gave me the strength to stand up for myself, not just in business, but for me as a whole being and for others who had or were suffering as I had.

After our divorce, I continued in Christian counseling, and I am thankful for an eye-opening revelation. I had known this preacher for about five years, and he had known my now ex-husband as well. He looked me straight in the eye and said, "When you begin dating again, or if you should ever remarry, you must find someone as strong as you are."

This was the best personal advice I ever received. Looking back, I saw that I needed someone that would let me be who I truly am. I realized that because I was strong in the workplace, I was being forced to change and step back in my personal life in order to conform to the person they wanted me to be so that they might feel better about themselves.

One can never feel better about themselves at another person's expense. This was especially important for me to reinforce as a mother of daughters.

LESSONS TO SOAR

Be willing to reveal who you really are. True grit comes from being true to yourself, and making no apologies for it. Stepping into who you are and were meant to be is when it gets really exciting.

Appreciate the cultural nuances of others. Customs and traditions open a world of understanding and opportunity when respected and embraced. Be open and appreciative to coming together amidst the differences among us.

Allow no one to minimize your strengths. Abusive and bullying relationships occur out of insecurities that are being denied. Don't allow another person's insecurities to cause you to doubt your talent, abilities, or values. Stand strong in your convictions and your abilities.

"When it seems out of reach, reach deep within and quiet your mind to see your options."

CHAPTER 17

UNI-SCREWED

A natural response for a salesperson when there is an opportunity in the air is an overwhelming sense of anticipation and excitement. It was no different the morning my VP of Sales at Victory walked up to my desk with a grin as wide as his face. I knew something was up and I couldn't wait to hear the details.

He had samples of a product that could revolutionize the industry. As I examined the samples, I realized you could use one size screwdriver for thousands of various sizes of screws. This product was a game changer in the fastener industry and I had to learn more.

Then I watched as he let his arm fall to his side, holding the screw still inserted into the screwdriver bit, and they would remain together as one unit. He did this for every sample screw he had, and the same prevailed. There were products on the market that offered some of these features, but absolutely none provided all in one. The cost savings to its users would be extraordinary in the manufacturing world. Its ease of use in maintenance areas and home use meant wholesale and retail opportunities.

A Game-Changing Opportunity

I was the most intrigued I had ever been with a fastener product. I thought this product could change how the world is fastened, and we could be the ones to do it. I asked the big question, "What does this deal cost?"

He said, "Three million dollars."

No wonder he was so excited about this opportunity. It would be my dime on the line, not his. That's when my ears rang with confusion, and my mind went into a tailspin.

While three million dollars was the answer I thought I heard, I knew there had to be more to it than just the asking price. I asked him to clarify more than once, "What's your plan to come up with the purchase price of $3,000,000?" He had no answers to that question.

That enormous figure was all I could think about for the rest of that conversation. No matter how much it would change my small business along with the possibility of overhauling the entire fastener industry with a one-drive, stick-fit system, how could I come up with this kind of capital? I told him I would do some research on the product and for him to get back to me the following day after lunch. I did a partial due diligence as far as fit and function, and the opportunity it would bring to the marketplace.

I simply fell in love with this product and its potential. I was a woman in a man's world, determined to do anything and everything better than they could ever do. The money was a hurdle that I did not know how to clear. This salesperson explained we could raise the money through investors, and he even acted like they would line up at the door to add this opportunity to their portfolios. I had never taken on investors in my career, so this was all foreign to me. He already had one investor in mind and the meeting had already been set up, so I was willing to explore further.

This opportunity took on a life of its own from the very beginning. The original patent holder was British, and the screws that had made it to market were being manufactured and sold in England. The patent owner was looking for a way to enter the American market so that the world would flock to manufacture and sell Uni-Screw.

When I first met the patent designer, I explained I thought the name was a weird name because it was a one-size driver system, not a one-size screw, but he explained they thought it was clever. "You see," he said, "the name could also be explained as 'You-n-I' screw."

With my back slightly turned to him, I swung around and told him that if he wasn't eighty years old, I would knock him off the stool he was sitting on. I was shocked that I said that, at first. I guess the "Marshvegas" in me had come to the surface, and I was so glad it did because that changed the course of our business relationship. He never made an offhanded comment to me again, as I earned his immediate respect. Our focus was on the business at hand. There would be times we would disagree, but that didn't mean we couldn't move forward. Many times, we would just agree to disagree, but we had a tremendous respect for each other until the day he died.

The owner of the patent, also British, and the designer were not "fastener" people and therefore needed to sell the patent to someone that understood the process and had the network to give it traction. Everyone saw the potential, whether in the business or not. Everyone wanted in on making the money, but no one wanted to do the work. Building a team with this crowd would be like herding feral cats, chickens, or anything else that absolutely cannot be herded.

I had seen many miracles in my life and career, but coming up with the money to buy this patented system was not His plan, even with all my prayers. In the infinite wisdom of the first investor and partner who came on board, he suggested I ask for a licensing agreement instead. This was a brilliant alternative. This same investor also took a 20 percent share of Uni-Screw ownership for his "expertise" without contributing a dime—clearly a brilliant business negotiator.

I had a meeting set up with the patent owner to buy the patent, and I didn't alert him to anything different before the meeting. Sitting in an upscale restaurant in Orlando, Florida—against my policy of no dinner meetings alone—I sprang the option of a licensing agreement instead. His reaction was one of utter shock when he thought I was there to sign the agreement to purchase the patents and to add $3,000,000 to his bank account. The meeting ended politely and abruptly—not the positive outcome at all I had anticipated!

A Milk Chaser

I left that night to drive the one and a half hours back to my hotel room to a sleepless night, where I had a boat show to work the following day. As I drove, my dad called and asked how it went. I said, "Not too well. So I'm drinking and driving."

My daddy yelled, "Renee, you know better!"

"Dad, stop freaking out!"

I saw a "Hot Donut" neon sign and whipped in for a dozen with milk. I ate eight. Even though I knew it would be worse than a hangover because I'm allergic to yeast, what the heck! No one except me is in danger and it tasted great. Whether celebrating or drowning my sorrows, hot donuts and milk always seemed to work for me.

I worked at the show booth the following day with many prayers and told myself that when God closes a door, He opens a window. I saw this as a blessing. Late in the day, I got a call and the window had opened. The patent owner was willing to do the licensing agreement of $500,000 minimum per year.

I wasn't expecting the call, but I had prayed all night that if it was meant to be, the patent owner would have a change of heart. My prayer was answered! He not only reconsidered, he was excited about the adventure ahead. And why not? He didn't get the initial deal he wanted, but he would have a much bigger payday over many years to come—if it proved to be a success. We planned a lunch meeting in thirty days, this time in Asheville, North Carolina, where we would sign the licensing agreement and confirm a wire into his account for $500,000.00.

The second I drove away from the meeting I had so many mixed emotions, I was smiling, my heart was racing, and the list of things to be done played over and over in my mind during the three-hour ride back to the office in Indian Trail, North Carolina. I even let myself dream a little about what this product could do in the industry. Everyone else had dollar signs in their eyes—which I did as well—but the guiding force for me was the victory to come for us to be known as the group to change the industry. The deal was complete. Was I terrified or elated? I was probably a little of both, and either way, the roller coaster ride was about to begin.

The first payment was due the day we signed the deal and would be every year forever. We had established a holding company that owned the licensing agreement here in America called Uni-Screw, LLC. Initially, the cost for the licensing agreement would come from Uni-Screw, LLC, which meant I would be responsible for the first payment, and later from the investors that would be brought in on the deal. Once there were signed licensees worldwide, and the product was in total production, the royalties would come from the profits made from licensed manufacturers of the screws and bits. And yes, I agreed to a

$500,000 minimum FOREVER! Doesn't it sound like a Mr. Wonderful deal from Shark Tank?

A Done Deal

The next few weeks were a whirlwind of meetings with attorneys, investors, and potential customers to begin building the excitement of the new product on the horizon. I met investors and partners from around the world. Since production and sales began in England, that was our first stop. Traveling across Europe was a dream come true. The various cultures were fascinating and learning that their way of doing business varied dramatically also made it more challenging. We developed partnerships across the globe. Not just Europe but Australia, South Africa, Asia, South America, and even in Israel.

Six months after I purchased the worldwide licensing agreement, we had signed contracts in place for over thirty licensing deals, along with distribution locations and manufacturers. My attorney's fees, salaries for everyone else, and travel expenses were rising much more quickly than the product was selling. I wasn't paying myself anything, and I told myself the hole I was digging was going to turn into a mountain of fame and money for the changes this woman was about to make in this man's world.

Once the partnerships were completed, they would each develop their territories and their sales would then pay royalties back to the company. It was a win-win. The product would be sold around the globe through an exclusive distribution network that we strategically developed. It was a brilliant plan that was established and approved by attorneys everywhere. It was a phenomenal deal. Well, on paper, that is.

When receiving small batches of screws from newly licensed factories, we discovered a disparaging gap between the products proposed fit and form, and what was actually achieved in production. Looking back, this would have been a great time to throw in the towel and obtain a lawyer to get me out of the deal, but instead, I pushed forward. I was determined more than ever for this to work. It meant going back to the patent attorney with a new patent design. I, along with two others from Victory Bolt, worked together to enhance the product for consistent quality. A patent listing our names as codesigners was awarded from the US patent office. Not only was it a superior design, we were patent protected around the world for an additional ten years out beyond the original patent.

The original patent owner paid the new patent fees worldwide, but I should have asked for so much more. I was on the hook for attorney fees, the time spent creating, the revenue lost while the new design was underway, and the list went on and on and on.

LESSONS TO SOAR

Align your team to win. No amount of hard work or perseverance can accomplish anything if a team is not moving in the same direction with common goals and a common vision.

Know who to trust. When the stakes are high, either emotionally or financially, trust becomes your greatest ally and asset to realizing success. The key is to trust those who affirm it, not those who expect it.

Demonstrate your resilience. Embrace your identity as the strong, vibrant, and valued person you were meant to be. Reveal the powerful person who emerged from what your adversaries enabled you to become.

5

LEADING THE EAGLE WAY

Most know that an eagle mates for life. Leaders face many challenges and storms; great leaders work diligently to nurture and protect long-term relationships.

"The biggest threat to your success is your own willingness to settle."

CHAPTER 18

WAR ZONE

The production of Uni-Screw had been moved to Taiwan for cost purposes and there had been multiple trips to keep things on track, both with the screws and the driver bits. The fit must be perfect for the system to work, bringing multiple challenges to the forefront of achieving the consistency desired.

From the very beginning, I felt the opposition from the owner of the European rights. It wasn't moving fast enough for him, and that meant a trip to Amsterdam for a meeting with his investors. It was clear that he wanted his investors to launch a lawsuit against me at this early stage of the partnership. After several hours in the hotel conference room, I demonstrated what was involved, the work that had been done, and the plan in process to get this product to market. At this meeting, the owner was told by his partners to back down and let me work. He was also asked what he was going to do to help the process in the European market. They instructed my team and me to continue the great work in progress.

War of Egomaniacs

The crisis was diverted, but only for a while. I realized I was spending a lot of time defending my abilities rather than using them to get the job done. I found myself in the middle of what felt like a war of egomaniacs—all with different agendas—and none were focused on getting a consistent quality product to market but instead to cash in and get out.

The European owner began to play a role in the process by hiring a gentleman that had worked in the fastener world for many years. He was based out of Switzerland and was very familiar with the European market. At first, it seemed like the right move until he forged a deeper wedge into our team.

A meeting was called. As we were sitting in a meeting room at a large hotel in Charlotte, I was feeling more and more defeated, and I spent those five hours in complete silence as I listened. In their opinion, my approach was totally incorrect, and a list of reasons why I was incompetent in launching this product took up an entire morning. I had been smart enough to have my attorney present and he and my partners were in utter shock because I said nothing to defend myself and I could feel their eyes on me—waiting for me to, well, be me. When we adjourned for lunch, they bombarded me with questions as to why I was so quiet. To my surprise, I didn't have an answer for them. I had no words, and I was just tired of wasting my energy.

During lunch, I felt I had no options left. My back was against the wall, and it was about time to resume the meeting for the afternoon session. I went into the restroom for a moment alone to think, and I prayed. Yes, and pray I did. I talked to God and told Him I needed help and He was the only one that could give me the wisdom to say what needed to be said. I also asked that He open their hearts and minds to the truth of the words He would give me the strength to say.

As I exited the restroom, the patent owner stopped me and stood about five feet from my face. He said that if I didn't do something, there was going to be a lawsuit, at a minimum of the European licensee getting his money back. He would have to sue, because the money had been spent to pay down debt on the work that had been completed thus far. This time, I did not falter. I looked him straight in the eyes and said, "Move and let me go to work. I'm ready. My prayers were just answered." He gave me a look like 'you have to be kidding me,' and I took a step around him and entered the conference room.

Into the Lion's Den

I took control of the discussion. First, I discounted all of their reasons for incompetence and reinforced that their mere opinions without details were unfounded. The tides began to turn. By the end of the day, a celebration was underway with marching orders on both sides of the table on how to continue the process and make it a success around the world. As we filed out of the room, my attorney patted me on the back and said, "See? You really didn't need me," and I laughed.

As we continued our celebration into the evening, I said to the patent owner, "I told you my prayers were answered, and I had what I needed to get the job done."

He said, "I don't get your faith, but I'm glad you have it."

And once again I prayed, "Thank you for answering my prayers." I hoped I was planting seeds of faith.

Screwed Over Again and Again

Problems continued to arise for the product. Either the screw was off, or the bit was out of tolerance. No matter what we did, the quality wasn't what it needed to be. When the screws were right, the delivery time was excessive as compared to other products on the market. Every day, I could see more and more that I was in over my head. I knew the industry and I knew the customers. I had never worked with individuals with nothing but personal agendas to only point fingers of blame, doing nothing to improve the situation at all. The plans from the previous meeting were not coming to fruition as promised, and I felt a lawsuit was looming over our heads.

I have seen in the movies and in the news where large corporations with very deep pockets would step in and stop some of the greatest inventions in the world if it infringed on their market share of standard and patented products. Well, I learned another lesson during this debacle that could not have been taught in a classroom.

No one, including me, realized the fallout that this would have on driver-bit manufacturing companies around the world as well as the screw manufacturers. Why would they want to help create a market for this great product if it would infringe on their current profitable business? Simply put, they didn't. In their minds, a one-bit driver would wreak havoc on the industry versus revolutionizing it.

I had another idea that could have turned this venture around. I thought, How about we make this product in America? I began working with manufacturers here to make the initial tooling that created the drive in the screw's head. That gave us more control over the tolerances and the companies here were more accessible for us to make changes and adapt quicker if needed. I was on a whirlwind looking for used equipment to make the screws ourselves, as well as working with an American driver-bit company that was very interested in the one-driver bit system because they had significant losses due to outsourced manufacturing in Asia.

With the help of a successful manufacturing company and some of my long-term relationships of expertise, this was going to turn around and this dream would come true. This time in my life felt like I was on a constant roller coaster, and with good reason. I learned very early that in the life of Uni-Screw, we couldn't get good news without bad coming shortly thereafter.

The European partner was growing tired of the time it was taking to get this product to market. The lawsuit hit my desk, and this opportunity turned into the biggest business adversity that I would ever experience. I was spending exorbitant amounts of money to defend myself and my partners. This was the beginning of a very long battle. The question was, Would I end up a victim or victorious?

Only prayer and God's timing could know the answer. It's still hard for me to grasp His power in what was to come. I would learn, however, that strong faith makes all things possible—not easy, but possible.

LESSONS TO SOAR

Keep your ego in check. In a war of egomaniacs, nobody wins. It becomes a battlefield of he said, she said, and nothing gets accomplished.

Leading takes courage. Outstanding leaders don't look for the easy road. They look for the high road and rise above the rest. Be willing to make the decisions that may be less popular and the least comfortable, knowing in the long run they are the right and best decisions.

Listen intently to criticism. Control your instinct to go on the defensive until you understand what is being communicated fully. Only then, if needed, can you go on the offense, equipped with using their own words against them.

"Attitude is a small thing that makes a big difference."

CHAPTER 19

THIRD TIME'S A CHARM

Dating after a sixteen-year marriage wasn't just exciting, it was also utterly terrifying. The single world had changed, and I felt totally left behind. Because I was always working, most of the dates I had been through had been people I had met through the industry. It had always been and remained my policy to never become involved with customers. A longtime friend, Kim, and I stopped at a local bar for a quick glass of wine before heading to a neighborhood annual Labor Day festival. The decision to stop led me to a chance encounter. A glance at someone with a captivating smile at the other end of the bar would be one of the best things that had happened to me in a long time.

I had spent my day doing financial planning at the Bank of America office building in uptown Charlotte. Susan was a woman I had been meeting with, and I certainly didn't expect her to walk up behind me as I stood at the bar. She got my attention and said, "Wow! What a coincidence meeting you here tonight after spending the day with you!"

Susan asked me if I was going to the festival. I said, "Yes, I am. But the band is setting up and dancing sounds like fun, and I am checking out that guy at the end of the bar."

"What guy?" she asked, and as I pointed to him, she said, "Oh, I know him!" and we made our way down the long, crowded bar for her to introduce us.

I learned Ray had seen me making sales calls at his former employer. He had seen me with the purchasing manager from time to time. This guy actually even knew my name because he had asked the buyer there who I was and was told I was married. That made me laugh. However, he also had met my ex-husband there when he was putting away our products into their manufacturing facility. My ex had indicated that ***he*** was the owner of Victory. So when Ray realized I was no longer married, he asked me what I was doing with myself these days? This implied that I was no longer a part of the company. I quickly realized what had happened and explained in no uncertain terms that it was my company, had always been my company, and would always be my company.

You would have thought after so many years of being asked if the company was really my daddy's or my husband's, I would have gotten accustomed to it. I had just finished negotiating the divorce settlement and after having to give my ex millions of dollars, I was a little raw with the subject.

After clarifying that misunderstanding, my stance did not faze Ray at all. He quickly understood my passion for the company. Ray said, "No wonder your company has been around for so long. You love what you do." I didn't see any intimidation in his face with the "attitude" I had just displayed, which got me to thinking he may have the confidence to be with a strong woman and that really sparked my interest in getting to know him better.

That night we ate, danced, and had such a great time. The bar and restaurant area had become packed with people. The dance floor was terribly crowded and while we were fast dancing, we were getting closer and closer. But then at about 11:00 p.m., it was like I panicked and told him I had to go. I still don't know why I behaved this way, except for the first time in a long time, I was relaxed and acting so much like myself that it was still somewhat new to me. After years of adapting to the person I was with, I think I was a little taken aback by just being "allowed" to be me.

As Kim and I headed for the door, I looked over my shoulder and waved goodbye. I had given him my phone number and headed home. I was in the process of telling Kim that I didn't even say thank you for the drinks and food when the phone rang. It was Ray. He wanted to make sure I had given him the right phone number. We both laughed, and I told him thank you and we planned to meet again after work later in the week.

Entering Ray's World

My professional life seemed out of control and there was never a dull moment with business at Victory or Uni-Screw. The following week was exhausting. Thursday was coming, and it surprised me by how much I looked forward to seeing Ray. That night, as we got to know each other a little more, he raised a question that I did not know how to answer. He said, "Tell me about your dreams."

Me being me, I talked about work and my goals for the business. He said, "That's about work. How about your personal dreams?" I realized I didn't have any and maybe I hadn't in a very long time. That's when he coined a phrase that still exists sixteen years later.

When he first said the words, I laughed and said you are such a "player." He had been single for eight years and was more accustomed to the dating scene. I can still remember the grin on his face as I said it and then he said, "I'm serious. Maybe you need to go to 'Ray's world' and dream a little?"

That night, I listened to his dreams, and they intrigued me. I had met a man with a kind heart that loved his family and friends, and I knew then that I wanted to spend more time with him.

I learned that he was a father of four and I met three of them fairly quickly. Our first official date was to a local high school football game. I met Madison, Jordan, and Zach that evening and got to catch up with high school friends I had not seen in years.

I quickly realized that I was standing deep in the county where I grew up and was again getting that small town all-eyes-on-me feeling. Not only did I meet people from my past, but I was also in the midst of his past too—old girlfriends and his ex-wife. I was being scrutinized, to say the least. At first, I felt it was a test of my confidence, but then I realized I had nothing to prove.

It was a fun night when we took Zach, who was fourteen at the time, and some of his friends to eat at Chili's after the game, and he politely asked, "Dad, why do you always date blondes?"

Ray said, "Thanks, Zachary!" as I looked at Ray and rolled my eyes. "What!?" "I can't help if I like attractive blondes!"

I looked at him and said, "You are cocky."

"No. Not cocky. Just confident," and we both laughed. It was a joke, but it meant more to me than he could have imagined. I felt like it was another reminder of the type of strength in a partner that I so desperately needed.

The following Saturday night Ray picked me up and we went to dinner. There, I would learn he had a fourth son named Josh living in Florida. I asked, how did he end up in Florida? Ray looked at me with a furrowed brow and said, "I've been wondering when would be a good time was to tell you something that you may not like."

I thought to myself, "OK, here it comes. I knew he was too good to be true."

Then he said, "I've been married twice."

I was taking a sip of my cocktail and almost spit it out. Then his eyes got big at my reaction, thinking it was going to be a very negative response. After smiling, I said, "Well, that tells me when and how to tell you something too. I've been married twice too."

This is a date that we talk about, and we have joked it could have been three-strikes-you're-out, but thank God, it would be the third time's a charm.

Down on Bended Knee

While on a trip in Charleston, he escorted me into a gorgeous courtyard surrounded by flowers with a beautiful fountain in the center. As we sat on the edge of the fountain, he dropped down on one knee and held up an open ring box. As I looked at him and the sparkling diamond, he asked me to marry him. I said, "Yes!" But I stipulated we would not set a date earlier than twelve months of dating. From my past, I had learned that many things can stay hidden within a few months. I had already made mistakes I did not want to repeat, and I felt a longer engagement would help us become even stronger together.

The next morning, I shocked my team with the news and they reminded me that there was never a dull moment with me on these trips. On one, I announced I was pregnant; on another, I was spending millions to purchase a brand new product system; on another, a divorce; and now, getting married. I told them I was glad they could live an exciting life through me.

LESSONS TO SOAR

Confidence is attractive. Once you surround yourself with people of like mind and values, your confidence feeds their confidence, and vice versa. It is no longer a competition. It is a heart-centered collaboration.

Dream a little to live a lot. When you are about all work and no play, your day is easily filled with more and more to do's instead of want to do's.

One year is revealing. In any relationship, things can stay hidden for months before they are fully revealed. You can be committed without making a commitment too soon. Allow time to forge an even stronger bond together.

"Don't wear yourself out trying to get rich. Be wise enough to know when to quit. In the blink of an eye wealth disappears, for it will sprout wings and fly away like an eagle."

—Proverbs 23:4, 5

"When you are too overwhelmed to think, stop thinking and start praying."

CHAPTER 20

JUMPING SHIP

Uni-Screw was getting even more complicated. I had moved into a separate location from Victory, which was a terrible decision because the managers I had left in place at Victory did not display the same level of service that our customers were accustomed to getting. This was apparent when I got a call for a meeting from our largest customer to explain the differences they were seeing. I had to repair the damage quickly before it could no longer be repaired.

Russ wanted to explain the differences they were seeing, and it needed to be face-to-face. He asked that I bring my current team, and he would get his buyers to attend as well. I spent one and a half hours intently listening. As all good leaders, the customer pointed out all the times we had risen to accomplish daily requests to seemingly impossible demands with ease. The customer stated we had accomplished much in the last fifteen years, and he knew we could get the service level back to his level of expectations. Last, he told me as I did my internal review to let them know if there was anything they could do to help or if there were opportunities to improve on their end.

It was as if my team had forgotten everything they had watched me do during their tenure at Victory under my leadership. From the most straightforward task of answering an email or voice mail the same day, even if only to say I am working on your request, to shipping requests being a day late—we had lost our Victory way. My customers had not felt served and valued, and knew that I would disapprove of the changes. I had always told my customers and employees, "I can't fix what I don't know about."

The ride home from the lunch in Knoxville was very quiet as I gathered my thoughts. The air was so thick with tension, you could cut it with a knife.

I became suddenly aware that this was not the only customer experiencing these issues. They were the only one that had spoken directly to me. This thought led to my pulse racing as my thoughts ran rampant into "what if land" yet again. What if I couldn't fix this? I realized my dream and vision were clouded by my mistakes and fears. I was too overwhelmed to think, and I turned to the only place I knew. I spent my time in prayer, asking for wisdom and peace throughout the process. I had seen God work miracles before and deep down, I knew He would again.

Getting Back on Track

As we got closer to the office, my mind cleared. I realized nothing was on fire yet, and though the embers around my feet were about to ignite, I would be allowed to rise from the ashes victoriously. I would use this adversity to come back stronger and better than before.

I had always said that Victory was like my golden goose for the success of everything else in my business life, and when it was in jeopardy, I would draw the line, and it was approaching that time. Through my internal review and calls to customers, I found that the issues someone had warned me about were running rampant. I documented every complaint with hard conversations that led nowhere and were addressed with futile excuses.

After a few months of juggling as much as I could handle, I realized that my only recourse was to terminate my two most senior managers. The very people that I thought were leaders had only led the Victory team down the wrong path. I had to be methodical in my approach moving forward. Dismissing employees was always hard for me, but I had learned over time that they had done this to themselves, and I had the future of many others to consider. For a few months, I juggled as much as I could handle, and then hired a new leader for Victory, one I could trust to lead until I could return to Victory full time.

Then I had another inspired thought. Could Ray and I work together? Our work ethic was so similar. He not only had a sales and customer service background, he also had extensive experience in operations through a management position at another distribution company very similar to Victory. I had been using him as a sounding board to the craziness going on in both companies and was thinking and praying it might be a positive move. I also had to get out of my own way in worrying that the past would repeat itself, having had previous romantic partners working in the business with me. He was different. He was self-assured.

He came into the Uni-Screw side of the business for a short time to experience working together and to get indoctrinated very quickly into my world. My world had gone from successful and fun to a chaotic and fast-moving, ever-changing array of one negative circumstance after another coming from all directions around the world. He, like me, was a fighter, and it wasn't long before he went over to Victory to get it back on track while I was flailing around in a Uni-Screw nightmare. This was the time in my life where I was earning my master's degree in the "school of hard knocks."

Getting outside Perspective

I had been participating in an executive level forum of business owners for many years. The group would meet the third Friday each month to discuss various topics and learn from each other. We could help each other avoid mistakes we had already made or learn how to replicate our successful moves. I gave them a very different perspective once I joined the group. There were ten men and I was the only woman. A few women came and went over the years, but I was the one that seemed to have found value in the learning and growth the group would bring in insights. It provided great perspective for me as I embraced learning ways to grow, increase profits, and to bounce ideas off of a room full of testosterone. Since most of my customers were male, it was extremely valuable to me. They often told me how much my thoughts meant to them because I added the heart, passion, and fun of running a successful business. It reminded them that at the end of the day, there was more to their business than just a strong financial statement.

We shared contacts and did business together within our various companies. It was like having an experienced, talented board of directors to help and hold me accountable for all aspects of my business. I gathered skills that still benefit me today and certainly got me through some tough times.

Annually, we had extensive four-day-long meetings that included our partners at all sorts of cool places around the country. From the mountains to the beach, we had fun at night, but we had day-long grueling training seminars with different topics every time.

It was becoming clearer each day that I had to leave the dream of changing the industry behind in order to keep Victory intact. I had taken out a second mortgage on my house and sold the building that Victory was operating in to try to make this a success. I had gone all in. What's the saying, "Go big or go home"? So many had believed in the product and had invested their hard-earned money, and I was devastated. I had gone big, very big, and I was about to "go home."

Ray came into my house one evening and I was sobbing. He knew what I was thinking about. I was always thinking about it, and he wanted to know how he could help. I asked, "Are you sure you want to do this? Be with me? It looks like I am going to lose everything I have worked for."

He came over to the island in the kitchen where I was standing and put his arms around me tightly and said, "Baby, I will live in a tent with you if I have to."

I leaned back and looked him straight in the eyes and said, "Please God, no, not a tent. Please let me at least live in a trailer like I was raised in." As he dried my tears, it brought a smile to both our faces.

Ray and I were married a few months later, the following September after we first met in late August the prior year. Our six children were in the wedding, and it was beautiful. We had a late afternoon wedding in a small historic white church near our home. The candlelight flickering in the original stained glass windows was romantic, and the feeling I got when I entered through the front door on the arm of my daddy and I saw Ray's face— I knew this was for life. The pews were full of friends and family, and it was truly my dream. We had a fun reception later where we played the theme to the Brady Bunch as we entered. After a week in Mexico, in a magnificent suite located on a sprawling resort, with the whitest sand I had ever seen, it was time to leave "Ray's World" and get back to my hard reality.

Dismantling a Dream

I finally had to admit to myself that no amount of hard work or perseverance can accomplish anything if there is not a team in place moving in the same direction with common goals, and when everyone has a different agenda, it is downright impossible.

The Uni-Screw location was dismantled, and all the material and records were reintroduced into the Victory location. It was time to concentrate on what I could do to maintain the success of what I had established so many years before. I had to make sure the faithful employees and customers that had made it a success would stick around for years to come. But the question was, *Could* Victory be saved? It had to. It just had to be saved. I needed to do what I had dreaded and stop fighting a losing battle with Uni-Screw.

I discussed options with a very close friend, one that I had met in the business group several years prior, who was also a Uni-Screw investor and strong supporter. He was a member of a group of investors that bought troubled businesses for a song and then turned them into moneymakers. We struck a deal that left my investors and me with 20 percent of the company and they would take it over. That's right, no money traded hands. I said, "Take it and see what you can do with it." It was such a relief the day they got the owner of the European rights to settle his lawsuit out of court in exchange for their expertise in turning this mess around.

Finally, I had good news about Uni-Screw, so I braced for the next bad news headed my way. Was I still on this roller coaster called life? I was about to see how this time would be no exception, in the worst possible way. And it would literally mean life or death!

LESSONS TO SOAR

Never back away from hard conversations. They provide the opportunity to improve, and in most cases, realize a more desirable result than originally imagined.

You can't fix what you don't know about. Be proactive in knowing how and what can be done better. By you. By others on your team. To know is to grow.

Get perspective outside of your inner circle. There is great value in gaining insights from those who have no skin in the game, yet they are willing to share their experience and perspective. Be open to it, and then it is up to you to decide what to do with it.

"Visualize a closed door as a window of opportunity. Your perspective is everything."

CHAPTER 21

STOPPED IN MY TRACKS

The same day I got the news that this investment company was taking over Uni-Screw, I found myself in an MRI machine. I was lying there praying, "Lord, please don't make me wait long to answer what is wrong with me." Amidst the stress of Uni-Screw, as months had ticked by, I found myself forgetting people's names, dates, and simple words were eluding me. Headaches were paralyzing and putting me in the bed every day by 3:00 p.m. only after taking a strong pain pill that just numbed the pain. No amount of sleep helped. I was always exhausted, and even the easiest tasks seemed like climbing Mount Everest.

True to my nature, I had to save everybody and everything. In the midst of holding the ships together, it had not been all bad news. I had kept Victory running and had actually obtained a few new contracts. Making sales calls had kept me sane because it was something that I dearly loved to do. I was also back in the Victory office and could mentor the team again. All the while, I was ignoring some things with my personal health that could no longer be put on the back burner.

Righting What's Wrong

My symptoms continued to escalate, with no known explanation, like the tingling in my right arm and leg. The doctor told me it was probably nerve damage from where I had broken my back. Then I was told the headaches and memory loss were probably my hormones. The fatigue and headaches resulted from working too much, and last, I was possibly suffering from depression and was prescribed antidepressants. The symptoms were small at first but were growing daily. Not standing up for myself and asking for more answers, I accepted the status quo, and it affected the long-term outcome tremendously.

Ray and I had been married for twelve months and he noticed the most significant changes in me. He saw the signs and was connecting the dots, so what did he do? He googled my symptoms and came up with his own terrifying idea, which he kept to himself, thank God. His diagnosis was multiple sclerosis. Ray went to the doctor with me, insisting that there was something wrong, that the behaviors were not like me, and affected my everyday life. He shared that when I was leaving work, he usually had to drag me out. But I was going home every day at 2:00 p.m. to take headache meds and then sleep until dinner. Then he would wake me, and we would eat, and then I was back asleep by 10:00 p.m. The pain never really went away. My memory was getting worse, and no matter how much I slept, I never felt rested. Ray demanded an MRI, which angered the doctor, who would later regret that terribly.

As I lay in the MRI machine, I asked God to please give me quick answers (you know, 'God, grant me patience but hurry, thing). It had only been two weeks since the MRI was ordered, but it had seemed like an eternity. With everything that was running through my mind, waiting a few more weeks would be tough. While Ray was thinking multiple sclerosis, I was thinking Alzheimer's disease. My grandmother had it at an early age, and it is hereditary, especially in women. The thought of not doing what I loved and defined me as a person being taken away almost took my breath away. I needed quick answers.

At Least It's Not Alzheimer's!

After the MRI, I got dressed and joined Ray in the room. We were shown various views of a massive brain tumor on the top of my head. They said it was the size of a man's fist and had been growing slowly for ten years. I was in shock, but Ray's knees almost buckled. The radiologist could not understand why I had not had a severe seizure, brain damage, or even died with a tumor this size. What happened next was something that I could not imagine. I was to be immediately transferred to the hospital for surgery—one that could lose everything for me, including my life. And yet, all I could think was, "Thank God it is not Alzheimer's. This can be fixed."

The day of the brain tumor diagnosis was a whirlwind. Being hardheaded as usual, I didn't want to ride in an ambulance to the hospital in Charlotte. I needed to let my mom and dad know what was happening, and hearing their only child was headed to the hospital for brain surgery to remove a tumor was not something they needed to hear over the phone. All I could think of was that I needed to head to Victory and gather my employees around to tell them and ask them to join Ray and me in prayer.

After a seizure in the hospital's lobby, things began moving quickly. I didn't have typical seizures like most people did. Tingling running up and down my right leg was something that was familiar to me, not realizing that it was actually a seizure. This time in the hospital lobby, it was different. It was like lightning bolts striking throughout my leg, starting at the top and shooting through the end of my toes. The pain was excruciating. Without warning, I collapsed to the floor. It was not only the pain; my leg was so weak it could no longer hold me. I couldn't stand back up no matter how hard I tried. Though it seemed like I had laid there for hours, it was only minutes until they were scooping me into a wheelchair and taking my vital signs.

Once I was safely tucked into my hospital bed, the IV was administered. As everyone gathered around my bed with eyes as wide as a full moon, I knew just how frightened they were. An hour or so later, our pastor came into the room and prayed as we all held hands. It was then that I realized why Ray's knees buckled when he saw the MRI images. He had lost his mom years earlier in a long battle with a cancerous brain tumor.

Our minds were in overdrive in preparation for what lay ahead. I realized as the nurses were making preparations and asking questions that I had no health-care power of attorney or an updated will. We were newly married and had never thought about these things. But, as they talked to me, it was apparent that this needed to be handled before the surgery. Being in business all these years, I was not short on lawyers to reach out to, and the paperwork began coming to my room for my signature via courier service. I didn't think about it at the time, but later joked that they must have seen the scans and thought I would die.

Then I met Dr. Asher. My neurologist had done wonders and was called one of the best neurosurgeons in the United States. I didn't know this at the time, but I remember thinking he's friendly, caring, and attractive. Yes, I thought that. I was trying to always look for the silver lining.

The more he spoke, the more comfortable I felt. Especially when he said, and I quote, "I think I can save your hair." I curiously looked at him, and then I heard my mom and daughters exhale. I had not thought about my having my head shaved, but everyone else was waiting on my breakdown. He came to my side, took his pen from his pocket and split my hair, and demonstrated how once he completed the surgery, I could comb my hair back over the surgery site. I remember thinking at the time that I didn't care about my hair, but he was right. That would have been something else to endure, and I was thankful for his kindness. Then, he joined us in prayer, and I knew God was again at work on my behalf.

A Different Plan

I was supposed to have emergency surgery the same day that the MRI detected the massive tumor embedded on the top of my brain, but that wasn't God's plan. My mind was running rampant as Dr. Asher talked about needing more time to review my scans to plan for the best outcome. My question was, "What about the seizures they were so concerned about?" He said that he would put me on medications to prevent the seizures and reduce the swelling in my brain and that it could be a few weeks before he could find the six hours needed to complete the surgery, and he didn't want to open me up twice since he could only book half the time needed.

That night in the hospital, I woke to find Ray staring at me. He was drowning in his fear and clinging to his prayers. I will never forget the look in his eyes. You probably are thinking we all must have been scared to death about what lay ahead. My head was spinning and yet what I was thinking while I waited was—no kidding—I have time to finish my projects at work and pass along whatever would still be in process.

I could call customers and let them know who would handle their accounts while I was away.

Well, once again, I realized I was not in charge. The medications were a disaster. One pill had my heart racing while the other made me desperately fatigued, even worse than I had been feeling for months. I felt like a brain-dead zombie.

All the while, the economy was crashing around us. It was the 2008 financial meltdown—the banking crisis that would be felt all over the globe, later known as the Great Recession. Everyone was feeling the pain, and daily I took conference calls informing me that Victory's customers were shutting their doors for good or mothballing them until further notice. They didn't care about any of my problems and projects. They were losing their jobs—jobs that they had for many years. I was so concerned for my employees and their families, and I was facing losing the company that had been my brainchild twenty years prior.

All I asked was for God to leave my brain intact and I would get through the rest. I could learn to walk again or even live without my legs, if that was His plan. Losing my life on the operating table was not far from my mind. Like a baby eagle that drops from a cliff expecting their mom to prevent them from falling to their death, I too would take a leap of faith and trust God to bring me back from this potential disaster, just like He had so many times before.

I spent much of my days in constant prayer because I could not go to "what if land." I had no control over either issue, and I had to trust or go out of my mind with worry. Ray was doing enough of that for both of us and half the free world. His world was changing tremendously, too, no matter the outcome. My choices were to worry about the company, which would have been devastating at any other time in my life, or think and pray about whether I would live or die during surgery.

I spent my time reading Philippians 1:21-24: "For to me, living means living for Christ, and dying is even better. But if I live, I can do more fruitful work for Christ. So I really don't know which is better. I'm torn between two desires: I long to go and be with Christ, which would be far better for me. But for your sakes, it is better that I continue to live."

The date of the surgery was approaching, and Ray orchestrated a prayer vigil in our home. He had three pastors there, many deacons, friends, and family. Our church, which at the time was the largest in our community, told him that our pastor probably would not come. But guess what? He did, and I joked, "You people must think I'm going to die." My bonus son, Zach, said the most heart-wrenching prayer that I have ever heard. Any fear that I had felt was all falling away, and I was ready for the big day. As I reflected on the verses in Philippians, I said to God, "I will be more help to you if you will let me stay." I had a peace in my heart that I would.

The night before the surgery, Ray made me his famous ribs that took him all day to make. They were so good! One might say they were to die for. I know it may be hard to see the humor in this, but that is how I tend to roll. That night I wrote a special card to each of the children, telling them what they meant to me, and went to sleep. I had made my peace with whatever happened. I was ready, but I saw the fear and worry in everyone else's eyes.

The surgery was supposed to take approximately six hours, with three to five days in intensive care and up to eight days in the hospital. Instead, it took twelve hours. The doctor came out with an update about halfway through and prepared Ray that I probably would not know anyone because of hemorrhaging during surgery and I may have had a stroke on my right side as well. The kids and my parents also had a terrible time during the extensive surgery. This news only made it worse. Would I make it? What would we be facing if I did? All they could do was wait, hope, and pray. Gratefully, their prayers and good thoughts were heard, and no one expected what would happen the following morning in the intensive care department, especially my doctor.

A Fine Howdy Do

In the recovery room, I could feel that someone was near me. It was my doctor standing at the foot of my bed. I opened my eyes and said, "Good morning, Dr. Asher."

He looked like he had seen a ghost. I had just shocked him. Dr. Asher immediately left my room to find Ray to tell him what had just happened. Dr. Asher said it was a miracle. He had viewed the MRI they had done at 3:00 a.m. and expected to see a vegetable in recovery.

Ray rushed into my room to hear me say, "Hey, Honey! How are you?" He sobbed like a baby. I had the easy part of sleeping during the entire surgery and much of the night—at least, sleeping between the pokes, prods, and throwing up from the anesthesia. It wasn't as bad as what he and my family had been through, worrying about me.

It wasn't long before I realized I couldn't feel my legs. I was paralyzed from the waist down. They would go into terrible muscle spasms and shake violently. Ray would try to hold them down on the bed, but we could do nothing to stop it. Even the nurses didn't know how to help until the physical therapy (PT) doctor arrived the next day. But there was one thing that did the trick. I would repeat the verse Psalm 46:10: "Be still, and know that I am God," and they would stop. Really!

My lower body wasn't the only problem. When they tried to sit me on the side of the bed, I couldn't sit up either. My upper body felt different. I could feel when someone touched me—unlike my legs—yet I could not hold myself upright. The day that I went to rehab, they brought in "Susie," a computerized/motorized machine that was large enough to lift me out of bed and stand me up. Ray looked at me while hoisting me out of bed and asked, "Why are you smiling?"

"With equipment like this, I will get past this, somehow, some way."

I have never felt closer to God than during this time, but there was still a big question looming. Was it cancer? The last night before they moved me to rehab, I heard a still small voice. "It's not cancer. Now heal." I awoke with a smile on my face. Early that morning, Dr. Asher came in and said, "Great news! The tumor was not cancerous." I smiled at him and thought to myself, "I know!"

When the PT doctor came in and heard about my legs, he explained he needed to get me over to the rehab hospital to begin my rehabilitation. I was out of intensive care within twenty-four hours and not the expected three days minimum. Then I was moved to a regular room, where it was predicted I would be there for about a week. Instead, I was headed to the rehab hospital two days later.

My battle, however, had only begun. I had survived, but what was God's plan for my life? What would life be like for me and those I loved and depended on me for so much? My faith had gotten me through the surgery, but there was so much left to the story. I had already seen God's miracles several times in my life. I had to hang on to that fact, believing He would do it for me again. This was more than I could handle on my own. God had placed me in a situation that I couldn't manage alone.

While many will say God won't give you what you aren't strong enough to handle, God *may* allow you to experience trials so that you will be in total dependence on Him.

LESSONS TO SOAR

God's timeline differs from ours. Patience is never easy for a high achiever. Your waiting might be preparing you for the plans and purposes God has in store for you. If you find yourself growing weary, look back and look up. Look back at what has already been accomplished and look up as evidence of God's presence.

You can't save anyone until you save yourself. When it comes to taking care of business, you must first realize that this means taking care of you. Your spirit. Your emotional wellbeing. Your physical wellbeing. Your soul.

Don't accept the status quo. Whether it is your health, your livelihood, or for those you love, stand up for yourself. Speak up. Demand to have answers to the questions rolling around in your head.

6

LEADING THE EAGLE WAY

An eagle is patient as it waits for the perfect wind to take the giant leap off the edge of a cliff, using its expansive and heavy wings to soar. As leaders, we must also learn patience to see the way forward amid a storm in order to see opportunities to survive and thrive.

"Be thankful for today, because in one moment your entire life could change forever."

CHAPTER 22

WALK, CAN'T RUN

Ray never left my side, and my family and friends were amazing. My upper body came back within about seven days, and I was able to transfer out of the wheelchair on my own. The staff gave me training on how to live in a wheelchair while in the rehab hospital. I began adapting to the long journey of teaching myself to walk again. It wasn't long before we realized I could not pull my feet up and I had what is known as drop foot. My physical therapy (PT) specialist would wrap the bottoms of my feet with ace bandages up and around to my calves so that I could use the parallel bars to take my first steps.

At that point, I was so thankful for the use of my upper body because I quickly realized that though my legs were moving in a stepping motion, 90 percent of my weight was being carried by my arms to help me move forward. Every night I had to sleep in these huge braces that held my feet upward so my toes would face the ceiling. This was in hopes that the nerve damage could be reversed. It was not long before they fitted me for braces that fit in my shoes to lift my feet so I could continue the process of retraining my brain to activate the movements needed to walk. The braces were so uncomfortable, but the pumps that were attached to my legs night after night for blood circulation were even worse.

I was doing physical therapy and occupational therapy. The therapist taught me how to do the once simple tasks in the bathroom with no embarrassment or hopelessness. After the surgery, they had placed a shunt to prevent swelling and to allow for drainage on the top of my head. I remember the first time they washed my hair after Dr. Asher removed the shunt. There had been so much dried blood it seemed like it took forever to wash it out, and I enjoyed every minute.

They taught me how to maneuver in the kitchen and I realized it was going to be very difficult because of the configuration of our kitchen. Ray told them it didn't really matter, I never cooked anyway, and we all laughed. I have to admit, it was true. The PT specialist would stop by and check on me even when I was not on her schedule. She was a kind lady that taught me what it is like to serve others while doing what you are called to do. And I will never forget the impression she made on me.

The workaholic in me was still ever present. I wanted to use my laptop so badly in the rehab hospital to reconnect with the office. Both Ray and I knew I wasn't able to just yet. I would ask him to bring it to me and he would say, "Not yet." It was one of the first times and probably the last that I didn't put up a fight to work. It was a blessing that I did not.

The physical part of the therapy, while it made me physically tired, actually felt good. But the brain game treatment was almost mentally crippling. When playing a beginner's level game, I failed miserably and finally the tears poured from my eyes. I got a glimpse of what would have been, if my brain had been affected like my legs were. As I improved every day, I quickly realized it was as they said, the memory lapses would get better with time. Once again, I was blessed beyond measure. I may not have been able to work then, but I also knew with all my heart that I would when the time was right.

After being in the physical therapy hospital for over a month, my physiatrist wanted me to continue my stay another thirty days because of the physical progress. As the doctor was waiting to hear from my insurance company, he noticed my anxiety and he asked multiple questions. "You seem so optimistic about your progress. Where is this coming from?"

"I need to get back to my real life to see how it will be," was my answer.

Home Sweet Home

The day we left was so invigorating. As Ray drove us home, I put the window down and felt the breeze on my face. I felt like things were a little more normal, but I would learn soon enough that wasn't exactly true. As we drove down the highway, I spotted a green sign with red letters. Then I saw bright neon lights flicker "HOT DONUTS NOW." Yes, it was Krispy Kreme. Ray did a U-turn and we pulled in and went through the drive through. My taste buds were in high gear as I was scarfing down my portion of the dozen glazed donuts that were melting in my mouth. This was a fantastic diversion from what I would experience when I got home. As you can tell, I ***really*** love Krispy Kreme donuts!

Everything in the hospital was perfect for life in a wheelchair. At home, not so much. My wheelchair would fit into the bathroom, but not into the toilet room. There was a raised lip in the shower, therefore not wheelchair accessible. I couldn't get into the half bath either. Ray was under tremendous physical and mental stress from my total dependence on him. He would regularly have to pick me up and move me from the wheelchair for my basic care. Ray spent the next six months caring for my every need. He even had to dress me down to tying my shoes. He had to lift me into our bed because it was too high to transfer from my chair. Ray still loved me and never once made me feel like a burden. God has blessed me not only with a husband, but a best friend and a true partner in life. He is truly the love of my life, and I am forever grateful.

As I learned to walk again, the company was in total distress. In September of that year, the entire US economy stopped in its tracks. We were in the Great Recession of 2008, and it was like turning off a fire hydrant. The country experienced the biggest quarterly drop in fifty years in the third quarter alone. First, the housing market bubble burst, followed by a loss of seven hundred thousand jobs in the last two months of the year.

There was no product moving out of my warehouse, and mill shipments were still arriving that were placed months before the crisis. Our million-dollar line of credit was maxed out and my payables were growing larger every day, while my receivables were dwindling.

We went from forty-eight people in Union County and across the country to eight team members in Indian Trail, including Ray and me. I could not worry about this and get well. So I chose to stay continuously in prayer and to not go to "what if land."

LESSONS TO SOAR

Work with what you have. The times when you feel the most limited are when you must deeply embrace what you currently have despite the challenge before you. Out of appreciation comes renewed energy and determination.

Words are powerful. Positive self-esteem is invaluable to your well-being. Surrounding yourself with those that allow you to have an uplifting attitude and self-assured nature without working to tear you down to their level is key to living your best life. Never forget, words are powerful. The power of words—they can hurt or motivate. Use them wisely.

Perspective requires focusing inward. When it seems nothing is working the way it used to, you must find a place within yourself to accept that the way things are going to work now is different. Then and only then will you see your opportunities.

"Like an eagle that rouses her chick and hovers over her young, so he spreads his wings to take them up and carried them safely with his pinions."

—Deut. 32:11

"Clear vision and passion do wonders for you as a leader and for your team."

CHAPTER 23

STARTING OVER

I was back at work part-time in my wheelchair four months after the surgery. It gave me some resemblance of my once normal life. Things were so different. I was the most dependent person I had ever been, and the company was a start-up again. But I was also thankful I was there and there was still the opportunity to turn things back around.

I decided the only thing left was to repeat the early beginnings, just like in 1988. We had to reinvent ourselves and at this point, there was only one way to go and that was up. I was in outpatient rehab four to five times per week. Amazingly, I enjoyed rehab—not only was I making headway, it allowed me to tell my story and tell others at physical therapy, "If I can do it, you can too."

Turning Things Around

Pulling Victory out of this nightmare was by no means an easy task. It involved so many moving parts and that, along with my personal battle, seemed insurmountable at times. Then, once again, God came to the rescue and sent Ray and me an individual with a talent like no other. His name was Paul and he helped us to change our course to one that would make us more successful than we had ever been before.

Paul had once worked at a very large bank where he was trained to turn around their struggling customers that were in jeopardy of defaulting on their loans from the bank—aka "Turnaround Expert." Paul was a true entrepreneur at heart, which led him to founding his own company to assist small businesses as a part-time chief financial officer (CFO). His passion was to go into situations exactly like Victory and turn things around.

That first year in a wheelchair was eye-opening. I couldn't believe how I was treated. Everyone doesn't have the kind of support I did and that is still hard for me to accept to this day. People didn't mean to be unkind; they just didn't know how to respond. Mostly they spoke to Ray as if I wasn't there and the worst was not making eye contact with me. That instantly led me to thoughts of helping others understand what this feels like and make those who are physically challenged feel included in all aspects of life as equal to everyone.

As I advanced from the chair to a walker and later to a cane, seeing customers again and visiting their plants had me soaring higher than I had gone in many months. It was an exciting time for me. Even though I was still struggling, at least I was still here on this earth, and I was walking—slowly and with assistance, but I was walking! The customers were kind and supportive, which had been an enormous concern of mine. Would they, like others, treat me differently? Fortunately, they saw me as a fighter and knew that I would still be around to work with them in the same fashion that we always had. As I was improving personally, the Victory team was growing again and there was less pressure for Ray and me to manage it all on our own.

At this point, Paul was full time because, let's face it, there was a lot to turn around. I was learning quickly that there is a vast difference between a CFO that acts as a controller and a CFO with a vision to succeed. Rather than an attitude of 'we can't,' Paul had an attitude of 'let's figure it out.' He allowed me to take potential opportunities and find ways to fund them. Without growth, you will wither and die, and I had thought a few times we were at death's door.

As the economy was building momentum, I spent countless hours trying to move inventory from my warehouse that had been sitting for over six months. I desperately needed cash! The banking industry took a tremendously hard hit during this time, and while our bank had been willing to work with us, Paul knew it was only a matter of time and he warned us about what was looming ahead.

I was becoming more independent and could walk unassisted. My doctor said he could correct the deformities in my right foot and leg.

During the healing process as the nerves reconnected my brain to my body, my left leg came back whole, but not my right. My doctor recommended a surgery that would correct the deficits, but this one surgery turned into multiple disastrous surgeries over the next few years. Each one was less successful than predicted and would lead to another surgery to repair the damage that the previous surgery had created. It was a long road of pain that, at times, was overwhelming. I would think to myself, "God left me here for a reason and I have to push forward to find out what it is He wants me to do."

Sixteen Again

The day I drove a car again after the tumor surgery and multiple foot surgeries was a moment I will never forget. I felt like I was sixteen again. I had the music blasting and my convertible top down and for the first time in a long time, I realized just how much I had missed this independence. I had also learned that it was OK to depend on others, that I was not put here to do it alone.

I was driving home one day shortly after being back behind the wheel, and I received the phone call Paul had told us to expect. It was our banker and he said that as of the following Tuesday, our bank account would be frozen and any money in the account or that was received would be seized by the bank for our loan debt. No matter how much you are expecting bad news, it doesn't make it any easier when it comes.

We still do not know why, but Tuesday came and went, and the account was not frozen. It stayed open for almost three weeks. By that time, we had taken care of the issue by moving funds into another bank, which enabled us to continue to fight another day. Once again, I set up payment plans with our vendors, and we established an internal payment plan for the bank to pay down our debt to $0 within the next twelve to eighteen months.

As our manufacturing customers got back on their feet, raw material costs had plummeted. That seemed like a way for our customers to cash in, but our inventory had been placed at the market value over twelve months prior. As we negotiated, I learned that if I met their demands, we would lose money every time I shipped them any material, and that was before paying any overhead to process the orders. I felt like once again, I was out of options. Either way, I was probably not going to make it out of this mess. I felt that pushing back was the only choice I had, and that's what I did. It would be better to hold on to our inventory a little longer and pray that the prices would rise. We simply would not be around to supply anyone for the long haul while supplying at a loss.

Because I pushed back, the buyer I called said, "Oh no. We don't want to lose Victory. What can we do?" He knew that keeping us around was a win-win and would make his job a lot easier in the long run. He was a star negotiator for his company and was rewarded for cost savings. I'm sure looking back, he was thinking how much work, pain, and soft costs it would be for them to develop and implement another supplier.

I told him I had already explained and submitted in writing what we were willing to do that could be successful for both companies. He said he felt that the deal would work and that we could get together the following week in Knoxville for lunch and signatures. After thanking him, I quickly hit the button to end the call. I had some tears of joy to shed and some prayers of thanksgiving to offer. I could hardly wait to walk into the office and share the great news with the team. We just might pull this off.

Teaching People How to Treat Me

This instance reminded me of a quote that I had taught my girls many years before during some of the hardest times: "I teach people how to treat me." The buyer thought he had me at a disadvantage, but I had to ask for what we deserved as a top-notch vendor. He had a job to do, and he did it well. He knew that if he had to establish a new supplier, his career and his employer would suffer, and that amount of cost savings just did not add up. Throughout the years, Victory had demonstrated our extraordinary value and our respect for them and their mission, and that would win this battle and others that would be sure to follow.

We kept true to our mission by offering more than just fasteners through building relationships and offering solutions. I had always known my why in business. With the personal adversities I had faced, I was learning the why of what I do to thrive in my personal life. Down the road, however, I would see just how difficult it is to separate my "who" from my "do."

LESSONS TO SOAR

You can always start over. Remember that starting over is never from the very beginning. It is always from a new beginning. See it as a new beginning.

Empower those around you to excel. Whether at home or on the job, you are only as strong as the team around you. Give them what they need in support, resources, and can-do spirit.

Independence takes on new meaning. You don't have to do everything yourself. It doesn't mean that unexpected limitations take your independence completely away. It means that no matter what you have been handed, you make your choices with a clear conscience, a determined heart, and belief in what is possible with the support of others.

"There is pain to stay the same, and there is pain to grow; the one you choose is key."

CHAPTER 24

AVOIDING THE BUNKER MENTALITY

After the bubble burst in 2008, that little thing like a brain tumor and legs that didn't work, I had an eye-opening visit from Tom, the head of my advisory group. He knew me well, having been a part of the group with me for years, and noticed that things were amiss with me. I was failing to do what I preached and what I loved. As he put it, "I had a bunker mentality." I was waiting on something else bad to happen rather than making something good come out of the mess we had just survived.

What we needed was to come out of this abyss with guns blazing and with a new attitude. We did various things, and something for everyone. The offices had a complete facelift. We had little revenue coming in, so Ray and I and the rest of the team had a paint party to freshen things up and give everything a new vibe. They felt a sense of being a part of our "rebirth." We did simple things like rearranging the furniture, bringing in plants, and adding new lighting.

Getting My Groove Back

Later that same year at the annual Christmas Party, I was given an award. "Renee Breazeale, GOT HER GROOVE BACK." It was hilarious and so true. I did!

As the economy reignited, I was reenergized. With fewer employees, I could spend less time managing and do what I love—selling products, the company, the team, and the unique service program we had created. Once again, I had nothing to lose. We had come through so many storms and there were only two ways to go. For me, the only choice was up.

Over the years, I had worked hard at finding opportunities to brand Victory. Many industries, not just industrial fasteners, do not have patented and unique products, so we had to pave our way to distinction in very crowded spaces. Every day, smaller companies are being eaten up by larger global corporations. The spaces where we did business were crowded, and it seemed everyone raced to offer the lowest prices and cheapest "deals." If you are providing the same service and products with equal quality, as a small woman-owned business, how do you compete? How does any small business compete?

I remember the day when it was a benefit just to deliver our products on our own truck, and later adding a quality program added profit to the bottom line. Now, in the age when communication and knowledge are flying at us at an unprecedented speed, so much more is given away free as part of the way you do business. You are expected to have all the "bells and whistles" just to get a place at the table. So, the question that should always be at the forefront of your mind is how do I make my company stand out?

My chief financial officer would say to me from time to time, "We must be prepared. There might be another 911." I would tell him I couldn't run a business awaiting doom, but I understood his point. We always worked to be as lean and mean as possible, keeping expenses under control, keeping debt low, and profitability running high. How do you do this? Establish and work within a budget that allows for growth and opportunity, and one that is sustainable for a successful exit strategy down the road. While easier said than done, it requires having a continuous pulse on the business, the industry, and your own risk tolerance.

I knew from experience that what works well for you today may be different tomorrow. Your ability to react faster than your competitors will be one of the major differences between your small business and your competitors—especially the larger ones. When they need your product or service, they don't want to get your voice mail and hear that you will get back to them within twenty-four hours. They don't want you to contact them back with an email. That's what your competitor does. You must dare to be different, to make a difference.

They need help. They need your assistance. Your customer wants to hear in your voice that you understand them and are there to help. Your ability to hear their issue proves to them that you value their business. Then responding quickly to their particular need is a great way to make them remember you and your company, first, before anyone else.

Back in my groove again, we began rebranding ourselves. The company had shrunk dramatically in the number of employees, and I was in enormous hours of rehab and, subsequently, my mind was racing with new ideas.

LESSONS TO SOAR

Don't have a bunker mentality. When faced with a series of challenges in a row, it is easy to feel as if you are bracing yourself for the next bad thing to happen. Instead, focus on making good out of the mess you just survived to thrive again.

Work on your business, not in it. When you are a leader or a business owner, especially amidst challenges, it is easy to feel like you always must be in the trenches with your team. However, the best thing you can do for you and your team is let them do what they do best in the business so you can lead at a higher level of insight through working on what's next.

A budget allows for growth and opportunity. Too many people view a budget as limiting. It isn't. It is empowering for you and for those around you. With a budget, you know what you have to spend and so do others. With a budget, you have clarity.

"As you see change happening, be quick to change with it. Better yet, get ahead of it."

CHAPTER 25

CRISIS ADVANTAGE

While concentrating on building long-term customer relationships, we had developed a solution-based sales formula. Whether the customer had a problem, a new project they needed to get off the ground, or just wanted to get material more quickly than normal, Victory had become synonymous with the "go-to" company in a crisis. Perhaps all the crises I had experienced over the years personally and in business had fostered a business culture of resiliency in crisis management. Whatever the reason, it was becoming our differentiation.

Rebranding and our newly understood culture meant a new mission statement moving forward. It had to be short and completely define who we had become and would remain. Our mission: "To offer you more than just fasteners, to build relationships and provide solutions." We changed the look of our logo and all that went with it, and it was truly a new day. We had learned from our mistakes. It was time to move forward and find opportunities.

As part of our solution-based selling, over the next several years, we developed solutions and branded them using the Victory name: VictoryKote, which led to another unique branded product, VictoryShield and a few others. The coatings we offered had a slight twist on what others offered and we knew it was up to us to sell that difference.

Reinventing to Charge Ahead

As we saw the market changing, we were quick to change with it, offering new and better ideas on how to supply quality products and service better than our competitors. We wasted no time. Unlike the large corporations that moved like a dinosaur, we could pivot and turn on a dime. That, too, made us different.

Continuously reviewing our business model for holes and possible hemorrhages is what reinvention is all about. Complacency never serves a business well. The solution-based selling proved to build a strong balance sheet and profit and loss.

We were back and better than ever. Laid-off employees were returning. New hires were being made. New customers were coming on board, and we were more profitable than ever. We were at the height of the company's success and were very thankful, celebrating the moment, while not kicking back and getting too comfortable.

We were reinvesting in the company by accelerating productivity without raising overhead. New software, better inventory management systems for our customers, and automated warehouse systems and manufacturing equipment led to the best customer service and support in the company's history. With the advantage of using our woman-owned certification, everything combined to put us at the top of our game.

It Wasn't All Perfect

Ongoing health issues included multiple foot surgeries to eliminate pain, plus my leg brace not improving my balance—failing time and time again. Despite the doctor's best effort, the nerve damage created by the brain tumor surgery would be something that surgery could not overcome. I had to learn that my "new normal" was being somewhat dependent for the rest of my life, which was very hard for me to accept fully.

I have heard my entire life, "Renee, you are so strong," or "You are one of the strongest women I know." But, at times, that has only been on the outside. Sleep was a coping mechanism for me on many levels. Sometimes, I would go to bed for days and hide from the world.

When you are in pain from, let's say a broken arm, people can see the results. There are X-rays and a cast that prove there is pain. But when it is internal, especially when things seem "rosy" on the outside, there is no visible sign. Depression is one of those things that is hard for those that do not suffer to understand, and sadly, many suffer alone.

I was diagnosed with a chemical imbalance many years earlier. Medications helped much of the time, but for me, talk therapy has been the most beneficial. I have also read so many books on the subject. Although I have come a long way over the years, no magic pill or conversation will ever completely eliminate the downtimes. I have come to accept them as part of who I am and focus on being stronger today than yesterday.

I would often chastise myself with internal thoughts like if my faith was stronger, I wouldn't get depressed. Even when I was put on my first antidepressant, I spoke to my pastor about it. I will never forget his words: "If you were a diabetic, would you take insulin?" "Yes, of course," I replied.

Thankfully, these strategies, plus prayer, medication, and talk therapy, won at the end of the day or sometimes at the end of a few days. I would work hard to give myself grace and allow myself to accept this adversity in my life as a way to help others. Embracing rather than chastising myself for these times helped me become more physically healthy and mentally stronger than before.

You may not find yourself in a situation similar to mine. You may not be fighting for a company. Perhaps you are fighting for your kids or for your marriage, but even if none of those things are true, fight for yourself. I don't mean in the literal way, but figuratively speaking. You are worthy of having a better life, to be respected, to be loved for who you are and what you stand for. Fight for yourself and fight for others to help them achieve through what you may have already learned.

LESSONS TO SOAR

Being solution-focused is a game changer. With crisis comes opportunity. It starts with seeing the opportunities through solving problems that others cannot seem to figure out. Figure them out and you are golden.

Rise to the occasion through reinvention. Those who are constantly evolving are light-years ahead of others. Being better than ever means you are always striving to be better. Even a new normal has a next level.

Invest in your future. You cannot take anything to its next level, whether it is your abilities, your business, or your team, without investing in them.

"Be open to persistence and reasons for your own resistance."

CHAPTER 26

KICKING & SCREAMING

The business was booming and so was the overall economy. I was being approached every day by competitors asking if I was ready to sell the company. My answer was always a firm "NO!" My husband would say, "It's been thirty years. Are you going to sell nuts and bolts with one foot in the grave?"

A few years before, I had thought about the changes I would make to the company structure as I got older. None of our children were interested in carrying the company forward. I also considered becoming an employee stock ownership plan company, but this proved to be very expensive to establish compared to the number of employees and it was a risk that I wasn't prepared to take. Selling to a competitor didn't seem like an option either, no matter how hard I thought about it. To me, that seemed like going to the "dark side," and if they were really good at what they did, how had we grown so much competing against them? Last, why were so many of their employees looking to come to work with us?

My answer to Ray's question was always, "Probably! If I wouldn't sell nuts and bolts until I died, what else is there?" Selling myself and the company was all I had ever done. Then another option suddenly appeared. I would find out later that it wasn't their first attempt to approach Victory to purchase, but their persistence would pay off in the end.

To Sell or Not to Sell

One day, I got a call from my chief financial officer (CFO). He said he thought that a company that had reached out to him was a viable option if I was interested in selling the company. Again, my answer was, "I'm not interested."

Then Paul made a second attempt with the same question. This time it was followed by how much would you take for the company? What dollar figure would it take for you to consider selling the company? I thought about it, looked at the financials again from a different perspective, and finally called him and gave him a number that I thought could never be achieved. Paul said, "I think that is a good number and can I set up a meeting with you and their CEO." I didn't expect that response at all! I had very mixed emotions when I ended the call because, surprisingly, I had said yes.

We had the first meeting over lunch and the CEO from the potential buyer told me later that he knew I was closed off to any discussion about selling the company from the moment I entered the room. He was right. I had decided that I was only there as a courtesy to my team to hear what this man had to say, put up a negative spin on every positive notion presented, and close this door.

As I listened, I quickly realized that this man was not only the CEO but also a pastor. How many CEOs do you know working for a company this size who are also a pastor of a church? I'm guessing not many, and this made me curious. After I had thrown out the price tag that I thought could not be achieved, my mind had raced with other criteria that must be met, even if I would consider selling. Again, I felt no way this challenge would be accomplished. I would be very surprised.

This was another instance of reckoning about whether life was about being in the right place at the right time or divine intervention. I was beginning to feel the latter was happening, whether or not I was open to the idea. This CEO was speaking "my language," and I was shocked that I was actually listening.

I drilled him with questions. What would happen to my employees? What type of culture, quality program, and inventory system did they have? The questions went on and on. The most important questions for me involved the employees. They had to be taken care of and be a part of a unified team moving forward. After all, they were my extended family and they were hard workers. They had taken care of Victory for many years, and they deserved the same in return.

All of his answers were viable, and I walked away shaking my head thinking this might be the move I'm supposed to make. Was it time to consider an exit strategy? Time would tell if it would it lead to a victory. It's all about your perspective. It would lead to an exit strategy that many would consider a success, but it didn't feel victorious to me. It felt more like a death. I was losing a big part of my life. You might say I was losing who I was.

I was constantly introduced as "This is Renee Breazeale. She owns Victory Bolt & Specialty." The company was a part of my identity. Who would I be if not the CEO of something I had built from the ground up? I didn't know, and consequently, I would struggle, to say the least, every step of the way.

For All the Right Reasons

As someone who enjoyed the freedoms of owning a successful company, it was never my driving force in life. I always considered myself a mentor, a servant to my team, customers, and to my community. Therefore, selling just for a big payday was not what would influence me to move forward with the deal. I would waffle day in and day out, frustrating the few that were aware of the deal and making the buyer more and more anxious with every passing day.

Each day, my CFO would go ask Ray or he would pop into my office and say, "Where do you stand today? Do I continue to proceed with the due diligence as requested?" Both Ray and Paul had made it their mission to get us out of the debt that had risen during the 2008 era and my unsuccessful attempt to revolutionize the fastener industry. With the growth over the last decade, we had succeeded, so I had to ask myself, "Do I get out at the top of my game or reinvest in the company once again and keep it going another ten years?" This was a question that I simply didn't have an answer to but God did. He had directed my path my entire life, but this time, I wasn't sure I was ready to listen. I would tell Paul to continue to see where it would lead us.

This time in my life was agonizing for me and Ray in ways you can't imagine. My method of decision-making was never black and white or based solely on the balance sheet and profit and loss statements. Yes, I used my intelligence quotient (IQ), but I also used my emotional intelligence (EQ). Although our IQ was considered being the indicator of the highest performing companies, I have always felt that EQ had led to much of the success of my business. Yes, this decision affected our personal future financial well-being, but it would also profoundly affect others around me. Whether employees, customers, or my family, they were never far from my mind every waking moment. During this time of my life, I lost a lot of sleep, especially those nights that I would wake with moments of sheer panic at 3:00 a.m. Change was coming. I could feel it, and Ecclesiastes 3:1 would come to mind. "For everything there is a season, a time for every activity under heaven."

The Chinese tariff implemented in 2018 wreaked havoc on our costs and supply chain. It was a nightmare and took a toll on our ability to get products from China and forced us to be very creative in establishing manufacturers in other locations in the world. It had always been our goal to buy domestic first and foreign second. With the pressure to compete as we grew, our market share forced us into offshore manufacturers more and more throughout the years. So again, American-made was our first option for a solution to the tariff crisis. And as they say, "Rome wasn't built in a day." The US had become more of a "service" nation than a country of manufacturing facilities and equipment, and it would take time to ramp up productions and buy equipment and tools needed to fill in the gap of required material and parts. I realized tariffs were implemented to create more jobs in America, but that didn't make it any easier in our daily lives.

Once again, it was not business as usual, and the stress of supply and demand was enormous. In my world of sales, providing jobs and keeping customers happy, timing was everything and the timing of the tariffs would play a significant role in my decisions moving forward. But the real question was: By how much? I would remind myself that there is a season for everything, and this season in my life would come to pass—eventually. All the others had, and the "fun" would begin again. I'm sure it would—or would it?

We had diverted much of our material purchases to factories in the US and into tariff-free countries. We were struggling with on-time delivery performances, but material was arriving daily, and this problem would soon rectify itself.

While yet another business crisis was turning into opportunities, the big decision was still looming over my head. Paul would continue to check my "feelings" odometer and occasionally throw in his question, "What if there is another 911?" Do I sell what my children affectionately referred to as "my true firstborn child" or continue my passion for serving our customers and mentoring our team of dedicated, wonderful people? The only thing I knew was selling nuts and bolts as CEO of my very own company. I was Renee Breazeale, owner of Victory Bolt & Specialty.

When faced with these types of decisions in life and in your business, how do you handle it? I did a lot of praying and asking God for strength to do the right thing according to His plan for my life and the future of so many others. Ray and I spoke with financial planners. I looked backward and forward at the economy trends and the ebbs and flows of the company's history. Also, I had to take an honest look at my physical limitations. How long could I continue the pace at which the company and I had become accustomed? I had tried to take the slower approach and each time I would get caught up in the rush of that next "big opportunity." Then I would head out again, exhaustively, just like I had when the company was brand new.

I knew, deep down in my heart, the path that God wanted me to take, but I would be like Jonah. You know the guy that went the opposite way that God instructed and ended up in the belly of a whale? Well thank goodness, there was no whale, but I went down the path kicking and screaming every step of the way.

LESSONS TO SOAR

Strength begins with self-acceptance. Amidst being strong on the outside for others, you can be consumed with so many doubts swimming inside your head. Accept yourself with where you are in the chaos, in the journey you are on, and have faith in the power of prayer.

What you do is not who you are. When you find great satisfaction in your work, you can begin to believe your worth and value are attached to your work. You were who you are long before you began your career or your business. Find that person again.

"No matter where you are in life, there are always more lessons to learn and more room to grow."

CHAPTER 27

LOSING MY IDENTITY

Victory had been blessed with several large formal contracts and transferring them to the new owner was necessary to close the deal as proposed. Making these introductions was difficult because I knew at this point there was no turning back. Then again, it was still my decision at the end of the day, and if I chose not to sell, the customers would not be surprised. Once again, I had an "out" in mind. I would tell the customers that I was just too dedicated to them, the employees, and the company I had built to sell. But I knew these introductions were inevitable, and I prolonged the misery by dreading it every day.

Behind Closed Doors

Keeping this potential transaction private was the highest priority until all points were agreed upon and we completed 98 percent of the deal. I had been told that one of this size could take the better part of a full twelve months or more. For us, however, this would not hold true. It was a much shorter time frame because we could provide audited financials for the prior three years. Looking back, I know this was also a tiny piece of the puzzle that was by God's design. No matter the length of time, He knew I would be miserable, and He wanted me moving on sooner than later to the plans He had for my future.

Stress was the word of the day. I wouldn't allow myself to feel any peace throughout this process. One of the weirdest feelings I had was that of "cheating" on my employees. There were so many closed-door meetings, off-site visits, and strangers walking through the facility that were described as "production improvement consultants." I had run my company by creating an inclusive group of individuals that empowered them to learn, grow, and positively influence others. I missed the "team" I had built in making this big decision for the company.

The due diligence was well underway, and we were proceeding to the customer portion of the process. I began making these appointments by telling them I had someone to introduce them to and the meeting needed to be kept confidential. All the customers I was meeting with had our employees on-site much of the time, so this only added to my anxiety.

It's hard to express just how nervous I was when the day came to meet with Russ, a customer that I had known for the better part of my career. When I picked up the new CEO from the airport to head to the customer site, I was physically shaking. I was also literally breaking out in red bumps around the collar of my sweater. I was itching terribly and trying not to scratch. What a nightmare! And to make it worse, I wasn't even sure what outcome I was hoping for.

The meeting did not surprise the customer, not at all. Several of my competitors had already reached out to him and asked what he thought they could do to entice me to sell. He knew it was a hot market and that we were primed for a larger company to purchase.

Since all the current employees would stay along with the same services, the customer agreed to the contract transfer, and we all went to lunch. As I stood in the restroom trying to wrap my head around what was happening and looking at the redness around my neck, I laughed hysterically. I had gone into a meeting that hinged on a multi-million-dollar deal, and I had my sweater on backward. Only me.

The top ten customers were visited, and all agreed to stay with reassurances there would be no significant changes to their service and pricing. They were also relieved that I was deciding to stay on board as well.

Time to Tell My "Family"

The last hurdle was staring me in the face, and I was terrified. The day came for me to gather everyone into the conference room. I began by telling them how important they had been, not just to the company, but to me personally. There were a lot of tears, but their intent was to stay and see things through. At that very moment, I felt like I had done something terribly wrong, had made a mistake and for a few seconds wanted to take all the words back. They were my family, which they could remain, but in reality, they were not mine to take care of. Victory Bolt & Specialty had provided them a prosperous life with opportunity and enjoyment, but it was time for a change. Change is hard but is also good, whether or not we know it at the time. After sharing the news, I was relieved it was over, but I think we were all heartbroken and a little frightened of the journey ahead.

The day of the closing was uneventful. It was nothing more than a phone call where I agreed to sell 100 percent of the company that had been my life for thirty years. The CFO thought it a miracle when I said yes to the sale as people around the country listened to me. Since the paperwork was signed previously, the deal was done—no muss, no fuss. All that was left for that day were the tears—a lot of tears.

The first year after the sale was basically business as usual, as they had promised all the employees, customers, and our vendors. I was grateful because it gave me time to catch my breath and move forward into a new role. But as they instituted changes, it went like wildfire through the company.

Feeling like an Outsider

I found myself an outsider. The "team" mentality I had expected and been promised did not exist, at least from my perspective. The team was only a few top-tier executives and managers, and the rest of us were on the outside looking in, speculating when the next curveball would fly across home plate. This is not an insult to this company. It is simply the culture of many large corporations swooping into a smaller, more nurtured and coveted culture.

Morale sank, and the pressure from management to do more took over. I watched the team I had built spiral into a world of "that's not my job," which reminded me why I had a company like Victory in the first place. The financial statement and balance sheet were solely ruling the day. For many, it was the first time they had experienced corporate life and terribly missed what they had prior. But thankfully, once again, God would show me His timing is always perfect for them and me. I have learned that God is never late. He's never early. He is ***always*** on time.

I took a role as a member of the national sales team. Selling products, the team, and the company were my passion. I didn't want any decision-making, or so I thought. I thought I didn't wish to manage others any longer, and again, another learning opportunity arose to teach me how wrong I had been with that decision. I will always be a leader and a mentor. These are my God-given talents, and that was what was missing.

I was without the title of CEO of Victory Bolt & Specialty, and asking myself, If I'm not here, what will I do? I had learned over the years when to say no, not always as soon as I should have, but I knew pretty quickly that working for a large corporation wasn't for me. I let management know my intentions to leave and had agreed to a lengthy exit time frame.

However, I only made it for a short while. Upon arriving at the office one morning after a wonderful vacation, I walked in, found my office dismantled with thirty years of memories shoved in a corner, and that was it for me. I walked out with an email letter of resignation to my corporate boss, saying I resigned immediately.

Not my finest moment, but I think it took something that devastating to make me embrace and breathe a new life into Renee Breazeale.

In the meantime, I focused solely on being a wife and best friend to my wonderful husband, a mother to two beautiful young women and four wonderful bonus children, a grandmother to nine, as well as a daughter to fabulous, inspiring parents.

LESSONS TO SOAR

Change is hard, but it is also good. Whether or not you know it at the time, when it is time to move on or move forward, never forget how far you have come and where it can take you.

Know when to say no, or no more. Stand strong in what you will accept in treatment, how you are valued, or what you will or will not do. There is strength in saying no more, not weakness.

You have not yet reached your full potential. We are each a canvas ever growing in the masterpiece we will become. We are meant to learn continually, evolve, and reveal our richness in being who we are meant to be.

"He did it for me.
He will do it for you.
God will find your
Victory in time."

CHAPTER 28

FINDING MY WHY

God blessed me with a change needed for my future and the promising future of my family and employees. He knew the pandemic was coming, and God had a plan. The day that everything shut down, I thanked God for his timing and again cried, but this time with peace and contentment. Not for long, though, because I asked Him, "What's next?" He answered in a big way and laid on my heart a path that I believe can give Him the glory and show the world that God is the hero of my life. Who is your hero?

I am adjusting to not being introduced as Renee Breazeale, the owner of Victory Bolt & Specialty. Without Victory Bolt being part of my name and my being, who was I? Who am I? I struggle with it still, but just not daily—only occasionally now. I still have thoughts and late-night dreams about my life at Victory Bolt. To combat my moments of being a Debbie Downer, I keep reminding myself God has a new direction for me.

Many days, I am learning that it is not what we do that determines who we are. It is who we are that determines what we do. As my Memaw Mitchem would say, "Renee, you have to put wings on your prayers and soar about your daily life for you to experience God's path for you." As a teenager, I probably rolled my eyes and thought, "What are you talking about?" I would cherish these words as I grew older, looking and searching for answers to the age-old question: What am I here for?

While writing this book, I asked each of my daughters, Heather and Savannah, to share what it was like having me as a mother. I braced myself for their answers because I knew at times Victory Bolt was the child that was getting all the attention. This was important to me for a variety of reasons, especially since I was beginning to realize that what I am here for is to help other women soar amidst whatever adversity life may hand them. I asked myself, "Have I helped my own daughters soar?"

When I first read each of their responses, my heart sank as they both started out with the fact that my business seemed to be first on my list while they were growing up. This was a hard pill to swallow, but also an accurate one. I had convinced myself, like many men actually, that since I was providing for them, it was justified and necessary. It wasn't. There could have been a better balance.

But then, they each shared how I showed them what was possible.

Heather wrote, "I realized over time that she was not only building a business to help others, she was showing my sister and me that we could build a business on our own or do anything else we set out to accomplish .... I have learned from my mother how to never give up. She has taught me infinite strength and leadership, and for that I am thankful."

Savannah wrote, "Boy, am I grateful for my workaholic lovely mama. She taught me how to be a hard worker, and most importantly, pave the way for myself instead of following someone else's lead. She also taught me how to be a good saleswoman, and as a tattoo artist, that helps me every day. She did something that I think is almost impossible, which was finding a balance while raising me."

I am not sharing this to give myself a pat on the back as a mother. What my daughters may not realize is how often I have wondered how my being a workaholic affected them. And how I now know the many things I would have done differently in order to be more balanced.

Quite frankly, their perspective was what I needed to hear, from both sides of their experiences, to reaffirm my pathway forward. Both of these amazing young women are venturing out in their own business, paving their own paths on their terms. And they are going to show me a few things because of what we have all learned together.

The Beauty of Adversity

I know now that mentoring other women is what I am meant to do—helping them know their own power and strength amidst adversities that attempt to derail them. I know now that I need to share what I have learned throughout the journey that I have been blessed to experience. My true passion was not just sales, but being a mentor and a leader. To share my extraordinary adventures of success, as well as the failures, has taught me so much that I can share with others. I hope to help women from all walks of life lead with passion and to rise above and triumph, no matter the obstacles faced.

My new business's name is Victory in Time, with all net proceeds from this business going to the foundation that Ray and I have established called Victory Foundation. We will concentrate our nonprofit contributions to those that provide services and support to battered women; victims of sexual assault, child abuse, and sex trafficking; or organizations that contribute to the quality of life for affordable independent housing, mobility, and inclusion of those with mental and physical disabilities.

It's been twelve years since the brain tumor and enduring seven foot surgeries. While I am walking again, it's certainly not pretty. I am left with a drop foot and spasticity in my right leg, and a pronounced limp. Things didn't turn out exactly as planned, but I am victorious nonetheless.

I am walking in heels, though small clunky heels and not as pretty as I had worn prior. I have much of my independence back, but will never strive to be totally independent again. When you know you are never alone, you can stand tall and know that there is so much to life and living.

I am reminded of 2 Corinthians 12:7: "Even though I have received such wonderful revelations from God. So to keep me from becoming proud, I was given a thorn in my flesh, a messenger from Satan to torment me and keep me from becoming proud." I'm in no way comparing myself to the goodness of Paul, but my limp is like Paul's thorn. God allowed this to happen to me to make me see the world and myself from an entirely different perspective.

Some days, I have pain in my right leg and foot that makes it difficult to walk, and traveling is no longer the joy it once was. One thing is for sure, I will never run again. The joke around my house is that not running is no big deal. Ray says, "You never did before."

My comeback is, "True, but I have always walked with a purpose."

Despite all of this, my prayers were answered. I rely on others willingly, but most of all, I rely on God. The best part is my brain works, well, at least as well as before. I am thankful and know that my adversities have drawn me closer to things I love.

My mission is to use my well-earned expertise to teach women to draw inspiring strength, courage, and success from every opportunity and adversity in their career, business, and life. And best of all, through knowing my why, I can help each and every woman know her why as well—starting with you.

LESSONS TO SOAR

Your passions fuel who you are. Everything you have experienced has impacted your life and others in your life. Doing what you love every day is the greatest gift you can give to yourself and others.

Turn your mess into your message. All that you have been through has brought you to this point right here. Your story and how you have overcome and triumphed could be what helps others and feeds your soul at the same time.

Faith first, not last. We are never alone because He is ever present. God can be the wind beneath your wings to soar. Because when you know you are never alone, you can have faith in yourself too.

"He fills my life with good things. My youth is renewed like the eagle's!"

—Psalm 103:5

ABOUT THE AUTHOR

Renee Johnson Breazeale is a small-town girl whose big dreams and faith in God started guiding her at an early age. Determined that nothing would stop her, as a native of Marshville, North Carolina, in Union County, she got the entrepreneurial bug early in her childhood by watching her parents in their textile manufacturing business. Graduating early from high school, she had her sights set on the University of Tennessee and moved to Knoxville, Tennessee, only to find that life's twists and turns revealed a different plan.

While working at a bank, an opportunity appeared for her to be a customer service representative for a start-up industrial supply house. Her love of the products, the challenge of being a woman in a man's world, and being in product sales drove her to learn everything she could about the business and the industry. Within a few years, she became part owner of a fastener business in Tennessee, and then in 1988, came back to North Carolina where Victory Bolt & Specialty was born—a 100 percent woman-owned business.

Over thirty years, the company grew to serving customers across the United States and exporting to Canada, Mexico, Poland, and Brazil. As a certified woman-owned business, the company earned the ranking of the thirteenth largest woman-owned business in the Charlotte metropolitan area, and the only woman-owned industrial business in Union County. Victory Bolt was also recognized by the industry as an innovator and leader for revolutionizing a more turnkey solution-focused approach to serving customers more efficiently and cost effectively.

Over the decades, Renee built her professional stature as an authoritative leader in her industry amidst overcoming personal challenges that included being a victim of domestic violence, breaking her back in three places, depression, and a brain tumor rendering her in a wheelchair. Never believing in the word can't, she defied her odds by walking again after multiple surgeries and countless hours of physical therapy, in high heels no less, within fifteen months. Despite these personal obstacles, she continued to forge her business into the industry forefront, surviving and thriving after the Great Recession until she sold the company in 2019 after celebrating thirty years in business.

She has given of her time, talents, and expertise as an advisory board member of Truist Bank (formerly BB&T), president of the board to Turning Point, Union County's battered women's shelter, which includes The Treehouse, a children's advocacy and sexual assault resource center, and Joni and Friends, a disability ministry. She founded Victory in Time, an organization dedicated to mentoring female executives and women business owners to realize their greatest potential as leaders, with all net proceeds going to Victory Foundation, a family foundation dedicated to funding nonprofits that provide services and support to battered women; victims of sexual assault, child abuse and sex trafficking; individuals suffering from depression; and affordable independent housing, mobility, and inclusion of those with mental and physical disabilities.

She attributes her strong faith in God and being surrounded by family, friends, and colleagues who believed in her vision as keys to her success. She enjoys making a difference in the community with her husband, Ray, and is proud of her two entrepreneurial daughters and four bonus children, while delighting in being the cool "NeNe" to nine grandchildren.

YOU DON'T HAVE TO SOAR ALONE

Throughout my life, I have been blessed with resources that have helped me cope and manage the adversities that were laid in my path. While an eagle is known for soaring alone high above it all, among the many things I am grateful for is me not having to be alone in these times where I had somewhere to turn for support, guidance, and options.

Should you or someone you know ever find yourself in a similar situation, please reach out to one of these options as a means of support and resource.

DOMESTIC VIOLENCE

For a Shelter in Your Community:
National Domestic Violence Hotline
800-799-SAFE (7233)
thehotline.org

For Resources:

National Coalition Against Domestic Violence
303-839-1852
ncadv.org

THOSE WITH DISABILITIES, THEIR FAMILIES, AND CAREGIVERS

For Resources:

Joni and Friends International Disability Center
joniandfriends.org
818-707-5664

MENTAL HEALTH

For Resources and Treatment Centers:
mentalhealth.gov

For Immediate Help:

1-800-273-TALK (8255)

ACKNOWLEDGMENTS

To our heavenly Father,
As the childhood song says, "When I am weak, you are strong. Yes, Jesus loves me." I am so thankful that you do. I am grateful that you chose me, your unlikely and undeserving child, to tell others what you have done for me and that you will do the same for them. Without you, I would have given up and given in so many times. When I think of the saying, "You won't give us more than we can handle," I know it's not true because you gave me more than I could handle alone. Learning to be totally dependent on you became many blessings in disguise. Forgive me when I let my fear overshadow your abilities. I thank you that your plan always prevailed, no matter how dire the adversity appeared through my mortal eyes. Father, this book would have a very different outcome if you had not saved me. I am eternally grateful. You are my hero. You are my victory.

To my husband, Ray,
From our first date when I saw the sparkle in your eye, to the moment when I saw your tears of joy as I walked down the aisle, I knew you were the one for me. Then, a short time later, when I saw your tears of sadness as you lifted me from my wheelchair, I saw in those eyes that God had created you just for me. You taught me to celebrate every aspect of our lives and demonstrated a love, friendship, respect, patience, and passion that I never dreamed was possible. Your loving encouragement throughout this writing journey made me feel incredibly blessed. Your belief that my life's experiences were worthy of publication has been the driving force to persevere with confidence so that this book can be a reality. For that and so many other reasons, I am forever yours. Just when I think I can't love you any deeper, you bring more magic into our lives, and the next thing I know is that I do! Ray, my man Breazeale, you are the love of my life!

To my parents, RA and Kay,
I am eternally grateful to you, mother and daddy, for the life lessons you taught me in perseverance and honor. Thank you for teaching me that failing does not make you a failure and that life after adversity is even sweeter and more valuable than some of the most significant victories.

To Heather and Savannah,
I am watching you become more like me every day, which is both good and sometimes terrifying. You are paving your own paths in life and I could not be prouder. I pray you will use your faith in God to never lose hope despite what the world says or does. We've been through a lot over the years, but simply put, I am so thankful that you will always be my babies and that you have grown up to be my best friends.

To my extended family, the team at Victory Bolt & Specialty,
Your unwavering trust, creative ideas, and strong values led to unbelievable fun, great memories, and many victories! I pray I influenced your lives as much as you did mine. I am incredibly grateful to have shared Victory with you.

To Dr. Terry Crimm,
I am grateful for your wise counsel and for all the times you helped me push my boundaries. I thank you and hope to have you as my counselor for many years to come (even though you're not cheap). Your insightfulness is never far from my mind, like your reminders to always stay in the moment and always put my real foot forward, not my best foot.

To Dr. Anthony Asher,
I would like to express my deepest gratitude to you. Your God-given talent as a neurosurgeon and skillful healing hands saved my life, and because of your kind heart, you saved my hair, too.

To Susan Emmett, my occupational therapist, and all other caregivers at Carolina's Rehabilitation-Charlotte,
Thank you for the compassion and support that led me down the path to understanding that even though my life may be different, I am still of value. You helped me know that no matter my limitations; I am to be respected, and that I could be an advocate for others with special needs.

To Sherré DeMao (BizGrowth Inc.),
Thank you for not only making this dream a reality, but for managing my crazy ideas along the way. Your entrepreneurial spirit was on full display, as your strategies kept me going when I was drowning in doubts during the entire writing process. We are truly kindred spirits.

To Fabi Preslar (SPARK Publications),
Timing is everything, and the fact that you came to hear me speak several years ago was perfect timing. That evening you heard me say my mess is my message, and you approached me to say, "You should write a book to help other women in business." Your little nudge helped me when I was ready to enter the next season of my life.

To all the customers and vendors that God put in my path to fulfill His plan in the life of Victory,
I am grateful. I appreciate your honesty, quality advice, your friendship, and willingness to take a chance with me and my company.

To all the women who have endured adversities far beyond my experiences,
I want to share my gratitude for leading the way for me and so many others to be victorious in our fight. You have blessed me beyond measure with your will to succeed and you gave me the courage to tell my story.

SOAR WITH RENEE

You can keep elevating toward your best life through reading Renee's blog, Soaring Heights, at **VictoryInTime.com**.

Renee is available to speak to business, industrial, charitable, and women's groups on a variety of topics, including leadership, sales, overcoming adversities, business success, and leading teams to excel. To learn more and book her for an engagement, go to **ReneeBreazeale.com**.

Follow Renee on social media!

in in/renee-breazeale-a895a27a

in company/victory-in-time

f reneejbreazeale

victory.in.time

VICTORY IN TIME

Building in Faith. Growing in Purpose.

Please note that The Victory Foundation discussed in the book is now known as ***The Victory Advantage.***

Helping individuals with disabilities or limitations live with dignity, independence, and confidence as contributors to society and as a part of the community as a whole.

Renee Breazeale
***Servant* CEO**

renee@victoryintime.com c.703-409-9578
www.victoryintime.com www.reneebreazeale.com
www.thevictoryadvantage.com

VICTORY FOUNDATION

Victory Foundation was cofounded by Ray and Renee Breazeale as a faith-based 501(c)(3) nonprofit dedicated to Christian teachings and principles. Net proceeds from Renee's books, speaking engagements, and Victory in Time will go toward funding the mission and ministry of their foundation.

All funding will be designated with special consideration to faith-based charitable organizations providing services to those in need, including (but not limited to):

- Battered women, and victims of sexual assault, child abuse, and sex trafficking
- Enhancing the quality of life, affordable independent living, mobility and inclusion to those with mental or physical disabilities
- Those suffering from depression

VICTORY FOUNDATION

To learn more about the foundation, or make a donation, go to **TheVictoryFoundation.org.**

"Yes, you will be enriched in every way so that you can always be generous. And when we take your gifts to those who need them, they will thank God."

—2 Corinthians 9:11

CPSIA information can be obtained
at www.ICGtesting.com
Printed in the USA
BVHW092021221022
649932BV00008B/28

9 781953 555335